REFLECTIONS
ON SACRED TEACHINGS

Volume Two: Madhurya-Kadambini

B.T. SWAMI

Copyright © 2003 by John E. Favors

All rights reserved. No part of this book may be reproduced, stored in a retrieval system, or transmitted in any form, by any means, including mechanical, electronic, photocopying, recording, or otherwise, without prior written consent of the publisher.

Hari-Nama Press gratefully acknowledges the BBT for the use of verses and purports from Srila Prabhupada's books. All such verses and purports are © Bhaktivedanta Book Trust International, Inc.

First printing 2003

Interior design by Subala dasa / Ecstatic Creations
Cover design by Brahma Muhurta dasa and Subala dasa
Photo by Brahma Muhurta dasa

Printed in the United States of America

ISBN softbound: 1-885414-14-5

Library of Congress Control Number: 2002109649

Persons interested in the subject matter of this book are invited to correspond with the publisher:

Hari-Nama Press
PO Box 76451, Capitol Hill, Washington, DC 20013

www.ifast.net/hnp

REFLECTIONS
ON SACRED TEACHINGS

Volume Two: Madhurya-Kadambini

Works by B.T. Swami (Swami Krishnapada)

Leadership for an Age of Higher Consciousness I
Administration from a Metaphysical Perspective

Leadership for an Age of Higher Consciousness II
Ancient Wisdom for Modern Times

The Beggar I
Meditations and Prayers on the Supreme Lord

The Beggar II
Crying Out for the Mercy

The Beggar III
False Ego: The Greatest Enemy of the Spiritual Leader

Spiritual Warrior I
Uncovering Spiritual Truths in Psychic Phenomena

Spiritual Warrior II
Transforming Lust into Love

Spiritual Warrior III
Solace for the Heart in Difficult Times

Reflections on Sacred Teachings I
Sri Siksastaka

Reflections on Sacred Teachings II
Madhurya-Kadambini

Reflections on Sacred Teachings III
Harinama Cintamani

Dedication

I would like to dedicate this book to all of the gurukula children who are struggling with obstacles in their lives. I pray that Srila Visvanatha Cakravarti Thakura will favor you with his blessings, and help you to rise above all challenges and obstacles.

Contents

Acknowledgments i
Foreword iii
Author's Preface. vii
Introduction 1
The Danger of Offenses •
Visvanatha Cakravarti Attracts Special
Deity • Questions & Answers

The First Shower of Nectar 29
The Cause of Bhakti • Krishna Submits
to His Devotees • Devotees are Spiritual
Warriors • Everything Depends on
Bhakti • Effort vs. Mercy • We Must Make
Ourselves Available • Questions &
Answers

The Second Shower of Nectar 53
The Science of Faith • Types of
Bhakti • Causes of Distress • Lack of
True Knowledge • False Ego • Material
Attachments • Envy • Mundane
Engagements • Neutralizing the Causes
of Distress • Bhakti Begins with Faith •
Unsteadiness in Devotion • Sudden
Enthusiasm • Lethargy • Doubts •
Material Sense Enjoyment • Unrealistic
Vows • Adoration & Distinction •
Questions & Answers

The Third Shower of Nectar 81
Understanding Karma • Sinful
Activities • Good Karma can be
a Distraction • Offenses to the
Holy Dhamas • Knowledge can be
Dangerous • The Misery of Falldown •

Anarthas from Devotional Service •
Offending Each Other • Breaking
Free • Trusting the Lord • Questions &
Answers

The Fourth Shower of Nectar 115
Sleep During Hearing and Chanting •
Speaking or Thinking Mundane
Nonsense • Feeling Incapable or
Disinterested • Acting with the Wrong
Consciousness • Attachment to
Sense Pleasure • Thoughts, Words,
Actions • Change Physical Actions •
Humility, Friendliness, Compassion •
The Bhakti Yardstick • Questions &
Answers

The Fifth Shower of Nectar 131
Conditional Taste • Unconditional
Taste • Questions & Answers

The Sixth Shower of Nectar 141
Questions & Answers

The Seventh Shower of Nectar 147
Sublime Meditation • Devotional
Trance • Revealing Bhava • Questions
& Answers

The Eighth Shower of Nectar 161
Developing Desire • An Audience
with the Lord • Overcoming Our
Disqualifications • Qualifications of a
Pure Devotee • Questions & Answers

Glossary. 197
Bibliography 207
Index 209
Author's Bio 215

Acknowledgments

I would like to sincerely thank Lila Katha dasi for the initial editing of the book. I want to especially thank Sarvabhavana dasa for his translations, which I have heavily relied upon, and Jambavan dasa and Jayadeva dasa for proofreading the Sanskrit verses. I would also like thank all of my disciples who transcribed the many audio tapes; and Jambavati dasi, Aja dasa, Kripa dasi and Subala dasa for layout, final editing and all the things necessary for bringing this book to press. I would like to express my greatest appreciation for Jaya Vijaya dasa from Australia and Rupa Manjari from England for financing the printing of this book. Let the *madhurya*, the sweetness of devotion, shower us all as we take shelter of Srila Visvanatha Cakravarti Thakura's unlimited mercy.

Reflections on Sacred Teachings, Volume Two

Foreword

Madhurya-Kadambini (Cloud Bank of Nectar), by the renowned Gaudiya Vaisnava *acarya* Srila Visvanatha Cakravarti Thakura, is a short work, and it is a commentary on an even shorter work—just two verses that appear in Srila Rupa Gosvami's *Bhakti-rasamrta-sindhu* (1.4.15–16). Merely two verses—yet they encapsulate extraordinary spiritual knowledge and realization. They set forth the sequence of eight stages that a sincere and serious practitioner of pure *bhakti* will ascend before arriving at the ultimate goal, pure love of God. Here we are given a valuable record of the factual spiritual experiences—from beginning to end—of devotees who have successfully traversed the path laid out by Sri Caitanya Mahaprabhu.

The two verses in question are quoted in *Caitanya-caritamrta, Madhya-lila*, 23.14-15:

> adau sraddha tatah sadhu-
> sango 'tha bhajana-kriya
> tato 'nartha-nivrttih syat
> tato nistha rucis tatah
> athasaktis tato bhavas
> tatah premabhyudancati
> sadhakanam ayam premnah
> pradurbhave bhavet kramah

"In the beginning there must be faith. Then one becomes interested *in associating with pure devotees. Thereafter one is initiated by the spiritual master and executes the regulative principles under his orders. Thus one is freed from all unwanted habits and becomes firmly fixed in devotional service. Thereafter, one develops taste and attachment. This is the way of* sadhana-bhakti, *the execution of devotional service according to the regulative principles. Gradually emotions intensify, and finally there is an awakening of love. This is the gradual development of love of Godhead for the devotee interested in Krishna consciousness."*

In *Madhurya-Kadambini*, the knowledge encapsulated in the two verses is opened up, like a many-petaled flower blossoming from a bud. Visvanatha Cakravarti gives an articulate, deeply realized, illuminating, and inspiring description of each stage. His remarkable blend of meticulous analytical reflections with intense evocations of devotional ecstasies is a singular achievement; indeed, it is what you might call the "signature style" of the *acaryas* who follow Sri Caitanya. There is a great treasury of world literature, gathered from diverse traditions and cultures, that records the varieties of experiences of adepts or virtuosos on the path of transcendence;

Foreword

Madhurya-Kadambini will increasingly be recognized as the most rare and precious gem in that rich collection. For those who follow the path of Lord Caitanya, *Madhurya-Kadambini* is an immensely practical guidebook. From it we can recognize at the outset of our spiritual journey that we are under the guidance of great teachers who command an immense body of knowledge and experience. Their wisdom and skill is awesome, and we can embark on this path with confidence and faith.

We must be grateful to His Holiness Bhakti-Tirtha Swami for giving us the work at hand—a summary of, guide to, and commentary on *Madhurya-Kadambini*. By drawing our attention to this exceptional book and by leading us carefully through it, he does a great service to humanity. People today are profoundly skeptical about spiritual knowledge and spiritual life, and their skepticism often becomes greatly reinforced by their own record of baffled and thwarted attempts, often undertaken under the misdirection of inexperienced, clueless or dishonest "guides." *Madhurya-Kadambini* is an antidote to such skepticism. Furthermore, Bhakti-Tirtha Swami, as a contemporary spiritual guide who follows the path of Visvanatha Cakravarti, shows how the process he describes is being conducted today. The conduct of spiritual life is best undertaken under the guidance of a competent teacher, just as learning to master the piano or the practice of medicine requires the hands-on mentoring of a skillful master. This work, based on a series of lectures on *Madhurya-Kadambini*, brings out the practical wisdom contained in the text, applying it to the conditions and exigencies we find ourselves in today. We see how the project of Visvanatha Cakravarti remains alive and current when it is translated into action by an experienced practitioner in the tradition. An illuminating and helpful question and answer session included at the end of each section is especially instructive in this regard.

Bhakti-Tirtha Swami has a gift for bringing ancient teachings alive to the contemporary ear and making them relevant to the preoccupations of contemporary conditioned souls. This is a result of Maharaja's personal realization. We should take full advantage of it.

    —Ravindra Svarupa dasa
     Vrindavan, India
     31 October, 2002

Author's Preface

Recently I received a very powerful book entitled *Children of the New Millennium* by a pious lady, P.M.H. Atwater, LH.D, who had several near-death experiences. She interviews young children who have had near-death experiences. The book shares their many powerful reflections and thoughts in relation to their experiences. Some of them recall their previous lives, and exhibit unusual abilities and powers that will unfortunately diminish if not properly protected or nurtured. In some cases, their abilities are not really understood or encouraged because these children might seem odd due to their insights, realizations, and perceptions. These days, there are unusual types of births taking place from both polarities. On one hand, we see children who are killing other children and are filled with viciousness, greed and other negative qualities, but on the other hand we see children with divine qualities. The fact that these distinct children are taking birth at this very unusual time in world history suggests something very powerful. Obviously the divine children have a significant role in bringing in a real new age, not a so-called new age still filled with the old archetypes and paradigms.

Many of these children shared certain dreams, experiences, or reflections that dealt with visions of their futures as well as visions of their previous lives. Some of these visions of the future at first included chaos, pandemonium, and confusion on this planet. They often saw themselves helping to inaugurate an era of more God consciousness. Obviously every parent feels that their child is special and will help uplift the world—and it is true that their children are special. Every soul is special because ultimately every soul is part and parcel of Krishna. However, some souls have very special qualities for they have descended into this world to bring love and guidance. Srila Visvanatha Cakravarti Thakura is one of these highly elevated beings who have come directly from the spiritual world.

Srila Visvanatha Cakravarti has not only given us this special book, *Madhurya-Kadambini*, for nourishing our devotional creepers, but his own life is a special gift to the world. Such great souls come into this world on a special mission. The pure devotees like Srila Visvanatha are conscious of who they really are, where they come from and where they, as well as all of us, can return to. They have some of the qualities of Krishna, for they expose the miscreants and they protect, guide and enlighten the devotees. They reveal obstacles and give us glimpses of the ultimate goal.

I am writing these brief reflections on sacred teachings as a way of helping and reminding myself and others how such mentors and their teachings, although ancient, are as relevant now as they were in the past. Let the *madhurya*, the sweetness of devotion, shower us all as we take shelter of Srila Visvanatha Cakravarti Thakura's unlimited mercy.

Introduction

Before I discuss various points from one of Srila Visvanatha Cakravarti Thakura's works, *The Bhakti Trilogy: Delineations on the Esoterics of Pure Devotion*, I would like to describe the extraordinary history of this great *Vaisnava* personality.

When there is an increase in sin, there is also a need for the presence of divinity. There is a need for more spiritual absorption and for spiritual personalities to counteract the negativity. Srila Visvanatha Cakravarti Thakura's life fulfills this purpose. Rupa Goswami, Jiva Goswami and Lord Caitanya had been gone for quite some time and, as in the time of Bhaktivinoda Thakura, *Vaisnava* culture was externally in bad shape. *Sahajiyaism* was increasing and people were looking down on this so-called *Vaisnava* lifestyle and culture. Furthermore, Vrndavana had become a sad place due to the demonic ruler named Samrat Aurangzeb. His regime was literally slaughtering *Vaisnavas*, breaking down the temples, destroying the Deities and raping the women. They even blocked passages and streets in order to monitor who entered and left. This was a very hellish period. Sometimes people think, "Just chant Hare Krishna and everything will be fine." Although this is true, it does not mean that there will not be any material difficulties for the individual, community or environment. However, the ultimate outcome is always auspicious because, although *maya* becomes extremely strong at specific times, *maya* is never stronger than Krishna.

Imagine Srila Visvanatha's devastation when he came to Vrndavana. He had heard about the powerful preaching, the building of temples, the increase in Vaisnavism, and the defeat of rascals, impersonalists, *mayavadis* and *sahajiyas* but when he arrived he saw that a devastating regime had seized Vrndavana. Many of the primary Deities had even been snuck out and taken to places such as Jaipur so that the regime could not destroy Them. We may wonder why Krishna allows the demons to gain such strength. Other people may think, "If Krishna does not even protect His most holy place, what kind of a God is He?" We must remind ourselves that the human body is designed for escape from the material world. This material world is basically an arrangement to accomodate people who want to forget Krishna to different extents. Srila Bhaktisiddhanta Sarasvati Thakura explains that this is not a place for a gentleman or gentlewoman. It is not a place where one wants to linger. One should do their business and get out. As *Kali-yuga* becomes more and more dominant, people will become so sinful that they will even start attacking and hunting those who try to propagate spirituality. Who would want to stay in such a crazy environment?

I received a letter a year ago from a devotee trying to preach in France; both the French and Austrian governments have declared our movement to be a dangerous cult. In such a place, it is almost

Introduction

impossible to get licenses or normal permits. The French government has made it very hard for devotees to preach. The government even encourages the citizens to harass the devotees who go out on *sankirtana*. One may think, "Why won't Krishna wipe out all of these obstacles? Why won't He stop their behavior?" Of course the religionists will think in this way. For them, spiritual life means that we should be peaceful and God should provide for our material gratification.

Of course, these devotees are not engaged in material gratification. They are trying to preach and serve Krishna. Devotees who try to serve the Lord often undergo even more intense challenges, assaults and attacks. Sometimes their lives are even threatened. This occurs not only to the *Vaisnavas*, but to many prominent personalities who try to propagate some aspect of religiosity or truthfulness. Jesus was crucified at such a young age and Muhammad survived several assassination attempts. The Muslim community still attacks Bahaullah who began the Baha'i faith. The Mormons were put in jail and beaten, and their women were raped. They were forced to move from one place to the next. Even Socrates was poisoned because he preached ethics and personalism, and Zoroaster was stabbed to death. There were several attempts on Srila Bhaktisiddhanta's life, and poisonous snakes were even put in Srila Prabhupada's room.

Srila Visvanatha Cakravarti Thakura was encouraged by Mukunda dasa, a very great associate of

Lord Caitanya, to try to help restore the sanctity of Vaisnavism. Srila Visvanatha Cakravarti Thakura was not an ordinary person. As a householder, he was always studying and absorbed in preaching about the Lord. Once his spiritual master had to personally ask him to go back to his wife. He returned for literally one day and night and passed the whole night preaching *Bhagavatam*. In the morning he left, so the spiritual master honored the fact that his whole existence was just for Krishna and for propagating the mission in such ways.

He had the overwhelming task of rejuvenating the entire environment, which meant risking his life and dealing with all the divergent philosophies. He prayed deeply for the capacity to accomplish this task. The *Vaisnavas* were bewildered about how to fix the situation. There was a great devotee at that time named Baladeva Vidyabhusana who was one of the major scholars and leaders of the *Madhvacarya-sampradaya*. The *Vaisnavas* often hoped that someone such as Baladeva Vidyabhusana could help preach the mission of Lord Caitanya Mahaprabhu because he was a powerful scholar. Even today the *Madhvacaryas* are great scholars but they do not honor *madhurya-rasa* or accept Srimati Radharani. So one great devotee named Radha-Damodara Goswami, a powerful *Gaudiya Vaisnava*, went to preach to Baladeva Vidyabhusana. In those days, people were genuine scholars and focused on both types of knowledge, *jnana* and *vijnana*. However, if someone presented a higher understanding, they

Introduction

would accept and surrender to that person. These were real *brahmanas* who had very strong arguments and put their philosophies on the table to discover the dominant philosophy. They were not just about social position—they were trying to be carriers of the knowledge and the message. When Radha-Damodara Goswami spoke on the intricate aspects of the *Vaisnava* alignment, which honors Srimati Radharani and Lord Caitanya, he converted Baladeva Vidyabhusana. Later Radha-Damodara Goswami sent him to Vrndavana to join Srila Visvanatha. Srila Visvanatha Cakravarti Thakura could understand that his prayers were being answered since he was receiving this very powerful *pandita* and devotee from the *Madhvacarya-sampradaya*. These two had the awesome task of restoring the *Vaisnava siddhanta*.

Srila Visvanatha Cakravarti had the tremendous task of trying to revive Vrndavana despite the chaos during that time. When there are great attacks, there is also a great chance to call upon Krishna. Difficulties can still arise despite Krishna's mercy. Although we can make arrangements to secure a situation, in the end it all depends on Krishna. We must work as if everything depends on ourselves but, at the same time, we must be ultimately detached knowing that it all depends on Krishna. This is how Bhakti-devi surfaces. We must act as if it depends on us but have the humility and knowledge to understand that we cannot do anything on our own.

Visvanatha Cakravarti did not think, "This is

insurmountable. Considering that Rupa and Jiva Goswami's arrangements have all been destroyed, how could I reestablish them? Let someone else take up this work while I write and pray in my *bhajana-kutira*." He did not think in this way. He did write extensively but he also went out to do the necessary. He intensely prayed for help and even teamed up with one of the top scholars of the time, Baladeva Vidyabhusana. According to the ordinary scheme, there would have been no chance for a top scholar of the *Madhvacarya-sampradaya* to leave and become a great proponent for Sri Caitanya Mahaprabhu.

At a later time, when Srila Visvanatha Cakravarti Thakura was almost seventy years old, a great challenge arose in Jaipur. Some claimed that the King and the citizens were making an offense by honoring Radha-Krishna worship. They challenged, "Where is there any mention of Srimati Radharani in the scriptures? Narayana is not associated with such. This is improper." Therefore, until they could prove this point, they wanted to stop the worship. The King was a *Vaisnava* but was confused and had no way to defend his position. Then they called for Srila Visvanatha Cakravarti Thakura to come and explain the position of the *Gaudiya Vaisnavas*. By this time, he had become quite old so he commissioned Baladeva Vidyabhusana to go in his place. Baladeva met these scholars, presented many arguments, and was even defeating them. Then they challenged, "As *Gaudiya Vaisnavas*, you are all under the shelter of

Introduction

Madhvacarya who honors Narayana as the Supreme. Where is your basis?" Then they explained that the *Gaudiyas* have no commentary on the *Vedanta-sutra*. Baladeva Vidyabhusana explained that we accept the *Srimad-Bhagavatam* as the natural commentary, but they were not satisfied with this answer. He then left in a very sad state but prayed intensely to Govindaji who literally appeared to him in a dream and gave him the commentary. This is a very special commentary meant to establish the *Gaudiya Vaisnava siddhanta* because the entire *Gaudiya Vaisnava* line was in danger. All of the great teachings of Lord Caitanya, Madhvacarya, Jiva Goswami, and Rupa Goswami could have been put aside. They were even prepared to take Srimati Radharani off the altar unless the *siddhanta* could be supported and defended.

The position of the *Vaisnava* scholars is to examine and try to understand the higher truths. This shows the power of Visvanatha Cakravarti and how he inspired Baladeva Vidyabhusana. The majority of Srila Prabhupada's *Bhagavad-gita* is connected with the commentaries of Srila Visvanatha and Baladeva Vidyabhusana. Therefore, when we read Prabhupada's commentaries, we are also reading the contributions of all of these great scholars. This shows their importance in our own lives as well. Srila Prabhupada explains that the commentaries of Srila Visvanatha Cakravarti would inspire him during great junctions or crises in his life. Srila Visvanatha Cakravarti explains that one must accept the order of the spiritual master as one's life and soul. After reflecting on this statement, Prabhupada said that he gave up all other considerations and focused on the words of Srila Bhaktisiddhanta in regards to preaching in the West and taking *sannyasa*. These personalities form an integral part of our meditation, history and existence, and our connection with such a great heritage is wonderful.

Srila Visvanatha Cakravarti's *guru* wanted him to make a copy of the *Srimad-Bhagavatam*. These days we have printing presses that can run off thousands of copies and we can translate the books into many languages but, at that time, they did not have these options. They wrote the books by hand, which made them very valuable and rare; therefore, people would find any means to study such knowledge. Now that we have so many books available, we do not really take them seriously. We have so many teachings that were not available in earlier times, and many great books have even been lost over time.

While Visvanatha Cakravarti wrote this copy of the *Srimad-Bhagavatam*, the sun would make itself available to give him light and even during the heavy monsoon months the rain would not fall where he sat. This shows Visvanatha Cakravarti's potency and the effect that he had on the environment. He was receiving blessings to perform his task due to the difficulties that he had to confront. Nevertheless, he remained enthusiastic to offer what he could. One night while writing in a cave on Govardhana Hill, he was reflecting on how to carry out these difficult tasks. Then, Lord Caitanya Mahaprabhu Himself appeared and requested Him to write commentaries on the *gosvami's* works. Why was this important? The *gosvamis* wrote in such highly sophisticated Sanskrit that even some of the *panditas* could not follow their meaning; therefore, Lord Caitanya Mahaprabhu appeared specifically to ask Srila Visvanatha to write in such a way that the common people could understand. Again we see this great teamship amongst the servants of the Lord and the different types of commissions given to each of the devotees. One may not have seen a need for any more books, since many books were already written but he was inspired by the personal instruction of Lord Caitanya Mahaprabhu to write in order to reach the common people. He honored that instruction and wrote over forty books in order to make the knowledge more available. Nevertheless, we see that this knowledge is still quite complex. We also see how Krishna Himself came forward to help His servant with his intense responsibility.

The Danger of Offenses

The life of Krishna-priya Thakurani helps us understand the danger of offenses. Just like Srila Visvanatha Cakravarti Thakura, she had literally no interest in the material energy or material culture. She was always absorbed in hearing, chanting and speaking, and people were very eager to have her *darsana*. One powerful devotee named Rupa Kaviraja had been trained by many of the great

Vaisnavas. He had traveled to many of the sacred places of pilgrimage, deeply studied the scriptures and spoke *sastra* in a powerful way. Once while Rupa Kaviraja was preparing to give *Bhagavatam* class, Krishna-priya Thakurani entered and many of the *Vaisnavas* stopped to honor her because they knew of her as a great personality. However, Rupa Kaviraja did not stop to recognize her and even felt disturbed so he just continued with his presentation. Rupa Kaviraja eventually became so angry with her that he looked at her with disgust and hate. At that instant, all of his luster and potency went away just as birds fly off a tree. He continued speaking but, after a short time, he started concocting all types of strange ideas. Since he was very powerful and famous, and connected with great *sadhus*, when he started speaking this distorted philosophy, many people joined him. He actually became a *sahajiya* and later he did not even honor or accept his own *guru*. Consequently, he became extremely sick with leprosy. This is a classic disease for heavy offenders. Literally his limbs just started rotting off and he died a horrible death.

This incident shows the seriousness of an offense regardless of one's position. The pure devotee at the highest level never makes an offense. Rupa Kaviraja was almost freed from *anarthas* and was actually experiencing genuine symptoms of love of God. He was one of the top philosophers at that time and had even traveled to all of the sacred pilgrimage sites. Even though he had intimate association with the great associates of Mahaprabhu, because he was so caught up in *pratistha* and in the appreciation of his own greatness, he could not honor or recognize another great person. He felt anger when he saw the other *sadhus* honor her. Therefore, he thought and spoke harshly at which point his credits were wiped away. Afterwards he became a ghost and could not even take on another body right away. However, he began to do wonderful service by haunting any *Vaisnava* who committed an offense.

We see the serious danger of offenses. Rupa Kaviraja, instead of joining up with Srila Visvanatha Cakravarti and helping with that effort, became like an ardent enemy. He began preaching bogus philosophy and consequently he contracted leprosy, his body rotted and he became a ghost. However, his actions began to remind others about the dangers of *aparadhas* since he would haunt any person who committed an offense. This became his service for some time. When an important person creates an embarrassment or falls, we can often trace the *aparadhas* that caused the problems. For this reason, it is dangerous for scholarly devotees because they often make more offenses due to their condescending mood. They think, "This person is just a *vaisya* but I am a *brahmana*." It is a very dangerous position. We see that many of Prabhupada's top scholars slipped away because they started questioning and doubting Srila Prabhupada. Several of them are now University professors who teach Sanskrit, Indology or comparative religion. Many of them were top scholars in our movement but, if we turn our *bhakti* into *jnana,* we will experience problems. We can check ourselves by examining if our knowledge is humbling us and helping us to appreciate the different aspects of *bhakti.* If not, we can be in danger like Rupa Kaviraja. Although he was a genuinely powerful scholar and *pandita,* we can see his actual fate. We must study with a sense of humility and always use the knowledge to help us become better servants. We can analyze how much we are becoming better servants by how much we are giving up sense gratification and whether we are becoming selfless. As we pray to devotees like Srila Visvanatha Cakravarti Thakura and study their works, we will be guided away from offenses and other pitfalls.

Visvanatha Cakravarti Attracts Special Deity

Once there was a first class *brahmacari* who had a very deep attachment to his Deities. Once the Deity appeared to the *brahmacari* and requested him to give Him to Srila Visvanatha. The *brahmacari* was dedicated and attached to the Deity but completely surrendered to the Lord's wishes. He went to Visvanatha Cakravarti and explained that the Deity wanted to be presented to him. Srila Visvanatha was very humble and not ready to accept the Deity who was so dear to the *brahmacari.* After the *brahmacari* took the Deity back home, the Deity appeared to him again and requested again to be given to Srila Visvanatha. Srila Visvanatha then had a dream

Introduction

in which the Deity explained why He was coming to him. Of course he then accepted the Deity. He also worshipped another special Deity, a very great *sila,* that had been worshiped by Lord Caitanya, Raghunatha dasa Goswami, and the powerful Vaisnavi, Krishna-priya Thakurani.

The *brahmacari* was a sincere servant, so when the Deity asked to be given over to another devotee, he did not hesitate. Although the Deity was most dear to him, he was ready to honor His wish because he was genuinely serving with his total existence. Therefore, he was eager to carry out any order of his Lord.

This is the real *suddha-bhakti.* It is not easy to grab or catch up with because we have so many self-centered concerns and mixed *bhakti* that we call devotion. These works are important because they can help us look closer at our current position and help us perform the work needed to come up to the unmotivated platform. This literature will increase our excitement in spite of the dangers or challenges, because challenges mean that Krishna will come through even more. For instance, once Srila Visvanatha was trying to figure out the *kama-gayatri* and was reflecting on Srila Krishnadasa Kaviraja's commentary in which Lord Caitanya explains that the *kama-gayatri* is twenty-four and a half syllables. However Srila Visvanatha was fixed in understanding it to be twenty-five syllables which greatly disturbed him. As a real *pandita,* he wanted clarity and understanding in order to honor and serve based on the *siddhanta*. Since he could not figure it out, he began to fast and pray. He was actually ready to fast until death when Srimati Radharani appeared. His life was amazing: Lord Caitanya appeared to him, the Deity appeared, he received the *Govardhana-sila*, and he received the association of Baladeva Vidyabhusana and Mukunda dasa. Srimati Radharani appeared Herself and explained that Krishnadasa Kaviraja was actually right. She then gave a very esoteric explanation that made him very happy and he continued writing amazing commentaries on these topics. When there is this intensity, Krishna will come forward again and again. However, there must be this intensity combined with humility, appreciation of the *Vaisnavas* and appreciation of the task. Without the combination of these factors, one can even come to an exalted position like Rupa Kaviraja but then become a ghost. Spiritual life is very serious and must be performed in the right way. These stories, pastimes and scriptures can help us understand what is what. *The Bhakti Trilogy* is one of the great works of Visvanatha Cakravarti and, as we hear more about his works, we can have a great appreciation for his connection with our *sampradaya* and a better understanding of Srila Prabhupada's alignment with so many of the wonderful great *acaryas*.

Questions & Answers
Question: In relation to offenses, I was a bit disturbed by an incident that recently happened in

a temple in Vrndavana where devotees were physically attacked in front of the Deities. If this kind of situation goes unchecked, does it actually affect the whole movement?

Answer: It does and already has. These types of occurrences are just symptoms of the disease. It is not that the symptom brings the disease but the symptom shows the presence of the disease. There are deeper issues. There are different reports but basically offenses have happened in one of the holiest places that should be filled with great exhilaration about spreading devotion. This helps us realize the prevalence of *Kali-yuga*, and if we do not develop a higher consciousness, we will also become a part of all this craziness in the material environment. It does not depend so much on right or wrong all the time but on serving and helping. It is not about who was really more responsible. For example, if your child is crying, you have a duty to facilitate that child. If women are disturbed and the men are supposed to provide protection, the men must find a way to protect. As proper leaders, we should deal with the fact that those under our care are not happy, satisfied or feeling protected. This alone is an issue. Therefore, the leaders must look closer at their dissatisfaction to understand why they feel unprotected. An important aspect of leadership is that the people under the leader should feel happy, satisfied and secure. We do not want to make people happy about sense gratification but they should feel happy due to proper protection.

This incident is a symptom of a deeper disease resulting from great dissatisfaction. For example, if you feel dissatisfaction or anxiety towards a person and you trip over a broom they left in the doorway, you might become angry. The broom itself did not cause your anger but, since you already felt some anger, the broom acted as a catalyst to cause a certain type of action and expression. This incident in Vrndavana just sparked a general feeling of anxiety since people sometimes use *Vaisnava* culture to justify the caste system, racism or elitism.

As we examine this incident more, we will find issues on both sides. However, the major issue still falls on the men because the men have the duty to protect. The fact that the women feel dissatisfied is a sign that the leadership is not properly helping them to feel secure. We find that people have been carrying issues for quite some time so, when an incident happens, tension immediately sets in.

The cultural aspect is more difficult to deal with. The Indian girls naturally have a different mood than the Western girls and Prabhupada honored both. After he came to the West and studied the situation, he understood the need for certain adjustments. If somebody does not understand time, place, and circumstance, they may have a big problem functioning in an International movement. We are not a unilateral society but we are a cosmopolitan society. Therefore, we have to honor the *siddhanta* but at the same time adjust the details so that the preaching spirit continues.

Introduction

Devotees have to accept that Prabhupada was not ultimately concerned with being Vedic but he was concerned with being Krishna conscious. Sometimes our conservatives or fundamentalists stress the Vedic ideal and quote from the *Manu-samhita*, but if they want to be honest, the *Manu-samhita* says that most should not even have the privilege of deeply engaging in Vedic culture due to their birth in the West and their absorption in the materialistic culture of sense gratification. If they want to honor some of the aspects of the *Manu-samhita*, they should honor the fact that they do not even have the right to speak. The *Manu-samhita* contains some heavy statements.

The whole idea of the protection of women is the same as the protection of the children. Protection does not mean that we abuse or exploit them with the idea of overseeing. We have the obligation as overseers and as servants to provide and take care of them. When we offer respects to the *Vaisnavas*, we emphasize the fact that we must honor all *Vaisnavas*, all generations and all genders. We do not create some type of sectarianism.

These mindsets always occur in the material world. People bring mindsets from their previous lives and develop new mindsets in this life. In the environment, they shed these contaminations to different degrees. Some people shed quickly due to their seriousness and some people shed slowly. We can study the scriptures to see if we are moving ahead or remaining stagnant. It is interesting to see how this situation has unfolded. The men created a line that blocked the women so the women tried to push through. We could simply accuse the women of inappropriate feminism, or we can look at the men and examine the reasons for their actions at that time. This inappropriate consciousness needs to be addressed and, if people do not address it, Krishna will smash them, especially in the holy *dhamas*. If people know what is proper but fail to act accordingly, Krishna will help them by giving them love in a hard way. However, when so many people feel dissatisfaction, it is a sign that the cause of the dissatisfaction needs greater attention.

    The *Srimad-Bhagavatam* tells us the results that occur when women, cows, the elderly and *brahmanas* do not receive proper care. Our problems with the cows, children and women must be addressed. We have *gurukula* children who are very dissatisfied because they feel that they were forsaken. Their parents were so engaged in the mission that they did not have time to take care of them; therefore, they feel ongoing disturbance, and some were even abused. In other situations, the parents sent the children away but they had positive experiences in the association of their peers and teachers. Other children had difficulties but somehow weathered them and remain positive. Some children are completely bitter. Some children did not even have any personal difficulties but, since their lives are somehow not right, they are furious. Some people just have not succeeded in their lives and they find a scapegoat.

Others have some genuine issues or problems. We have all of these situations.

We have these same results in all of the *asramas* and now with the women. We have some women who have given their lifeblood to this movement. Many temples would not even be here without their help in fundraising and organization because in many different situations the women brought in more funds than the men. Some mothers gave so much and now feel disturbed for many reasons. In some cases, they married a husband who did not work out. Maybe it was their own fault because they pursued such a connection. In other cases, it was improperly arranged. In other circumstances, they just did not have the *karma* for a healthy marriage. Some people can read endless books and visit numerous counselors but they just do not have the *karma* for a healthy marriage. For example, Visvanatha Cakravarti just did not have the *karma* for a successful marriage and so he left.

Due to such situations, we have people who use the experiences to justify their own failures. They are in *maya*. Now they campaign as a way to judge. They point out the *maya* everywhere so that their own *maya* does not seem so bad. They claim that the other *maya* caused their problems. We have many people in our movement with this mindset, men as well as women. Many people who follow the *rtvik* philosophy or other ideas have experienced disappointments in their lives and are not really following Prabhupada so they want to find a million reasons to justify their current activities. They may be breaking almost every principle so, from time to time, they feel guilty because they know so much. Then they claim that the *gurus* have caused all of their suffering or they find other issues to use as a scapegoat. Others are disappointed due to the *karma* factor in their lives. All of these issues continue but we can resolve them by considering ourselves to be servants of each other, and by seeing ourselves as a spiritual family, each with different, individual needs.

If the people we are trying to serve have a problem, we should listen and try to create a situation that helps them feel more secure or that alleviates the problem. However, many people will simply go on campaigns to justify their deviations with philosophical battles. Krishna uses *maya* to arrange many tests. Such tests will encourage the weak to deviate or engage in mixed devotional service. The same test will encourage the more serious devotees to make themselves stronger and to help in creating a stronger Krishna conscious family. Any crisis can bring the best and the worst out of anybody. Crises allow us to see everyone's real position.

Rupa Kaviraja's life shows the consequences of offenses that will wipe out your devotion and stagnate you. You may even come to the point of experiencing ecstasy or some connection as you enter *prema*, but if you commit some offenses, you can become a ghost just like Rupa Kaviraja. The way we deal with *Vaisnavas* is extremely important. So much of our existence is about the proper treatment of devotees. If you want to understand the growth and stagnation of different devotees, just observe their treatment of *Vaisnavas* and you will understand the nature of their lives.

Question: I would like to know more about the resolution of this problem concerning the worship of Srimati Radharani.

Answer: Baladeva Vidyabhusana convinced the scholars of Radha and Krishna worship. He gave references from many scriptures that mention Radharani and showed the esoteric aspects. He explained that Sukadeva Goswami could not deeply discuss Srimati Radharani because, as a great devotee of Radharani, he would have just gone into trance and would not have been able to finish speaking to Maharaja Pariksit. Baladeva Vidyabhusana could explain many different points because he knew the scriptures and could understand the deeper meaning.

Question: You just mentioned that certain emotions may mask the real underlying symptoms. I think that as devotees, if we want to mature and advance, we really need to analyze ourselves day by day. I personally find that anger tends to mask many of my other emotions, but if I take a moment to look deeper, I can get to the root of the problem and start looking for the solution. If we just stay on the surface, it seems that we will never accomplish much. Instead we need to take the responsibility to discover the real underlying issues.

Answer: This is the whole process of *bhakti*. Stopping the gross *anarthas* such as intoxication, illicit sex, gambling and meat eating is only the beginning. The real work involves looking at these more subtle *anarthas*. Real progress or stagnation depends on how much we are dealing with these more subtle blocks. For this reason, it is important to not only stop the sinful action but to also stop the seed of desires. If the seeds are still too strong, they will surface in different ways. Certain situations and conditions will cause the sinful desire to surface again. We examine ourselves deeply in order to destroy the subtle contaminations—this can be accomplished through replacement, *param drstva nivartate*. We can accomplish this by pushing out the nescience and bringing in more devotion.

Question: We see that Rupa Kaviraja had to take a ghost body due to only one offense. If our lives are just saturated with offenses and sins, is it inevitable that we will have to suffer severely or can we break the cycle and reform our lives?

Answer: For this reason, we must approach the people we have offended and genuinely beg for forgiveness. Chanting the holy name helps us gain freedom but we must simultaneously approach the offended devotee and ask for forgiveness. Furthermore, we must feel regret, repentance and the desire to change. Although we may have the will and desire, it must coincide with our speech and actions.

Introduction

We have to make the adjustment and beg for forgiveness in order to clear some of the negative *karmic* reaction. However, if someone thinks that they are not offending or does not honor another person's existence, they will not even see their harsh actions as offensive. They simply see themselves as God's gift to the environment and see their own actions as proper. Then they feel angry that the others did not recognize them as right. Humility is essential in devotional service.

In Vrndavana, they are having an issue with the women's position in front of Krishna's altar because the *sannyasis* cannot directly come to the altar and offer obeisances. However, if we are eager to see the Lord, why should anything disturb us? If there is a proper mood and people are satisfied, naturally when your father comes you would move to let him see. Or if your daughter is trying to see the Lord, you feel happy. So what is the issue? If you put these situations on the level of a family, then none of these issues are so complex. However, it is complex because many devotees do not even understand the meaning of a family. That makes it hard. People in modern society do not understand proper family life. They have not experienced it in their immediate families, with their parents or even with their grandparents. Therefore, they really do not understand the meaning of unity with diversity within a family. That makes it hard to try to create successful marriages when so many people come from backgrounds of unsuccessful marriages.

Statistics show that if a person's mother and father divorce, they are four or five times more likely to also get divorced. You could see this as a *karmic* influence but it is also a socialization factor. When you constantly see success, it consciously and unconsciously gives you the idea of success. When you see failure, it has an unusual way of impinging on your consciousness. The thing that you desperately try to avoid becomes a meditation and a mantra that you then end up manifesting. So many young girls come from families where the father was an alcoholic or obnoxious and, although the girl suffered so much in that environment, she ends up marrying a husband just like her father. Since she really does not want that same situation, it becomes a mantra and part of the consciousness until she literally draws a similar partner.

Relationships are very serious. For this reason, what we do with our children now is so important. Our actions are extremely important because we are either giving them strength or sending a message of failure. We must try to compensate in areas of weakness. The children basically need a male and female connection and, if we have children without male images such as a father, it is important that some of our men can be good role models. The actions of the mother and father are not the only influences, although they are the most dominant. It depends on all of our actions that add up to the child's experience. Many of the dysfunctional patterns in our movement stem from experiences our members had before they joined. It goes back to certain socializations and patterns that they have brought in and have not been able to fully eradicate since the *bhakti* has not become strong enough to check many of these problems.

Question: I was appreciating the previous comment in regards to anger that sometimes lies dormant until certain situations act as a catalyst. Many women in our movement have been abused or come from this type of material background. Maybe they have been raped in the material world and try to cover the pain. However, when they come to Krishna consciousness, they then have to face different types of situations such as the incident in Vrndavana. How can we be sensitive enough to assist some of the ladies in understanding their anger from the past and at the same time addressing the situation at hand?

Answer: There are many important points within that question. First of all, statistics say that one-third of the women in America have experienced rape. This is just how pervasive it is within our culture. This goes on dominantly when there is a mood of selfishness and a lack of caring. It increases when a mood of autocracy pervades and people feel that they can lord over what they survey. This happens in schools, companies or in any other place dominated by men. When men are in dominant positions without the proper consciousness, their minds turn to enjoying and experiencing anything under their care. For example, in Washington when women apply for jobs as secretaries, in certain cases it seems that they are being interviewed in the mood of a 'sexetary' rather than a secretary. If you speak with some of the women in these professions, you will discover that almost weekly they have to deal with improper behavior coming from their supervisors. This is all a part of material life. One would expect such in material life but might not expect the same in the spiritual community.

Furthermore, anyone within a material body brings in baggage from previous lives. We all bring in certain issues from before we joined the movement. Our earlier experiences have affected our present personality and the way we perceive or codify the world. We all have to constantly endeavor to counteract certain patterns based on conditioning. In some cases, it is more distinct or more distracting than others. This is a struggle every person must deal with in different ways. This is what conditioning means.

In terms of arguments, we have to move beyond talking and we have to really act. People cannot talk themselves out of things that they have acted themselves into. If we get too caught up in this kind of talking back and forth, it takes away from our ability to act differently. We have to act more in the proper way and let that prevail and help.

In this period of time, communication is just so accessible. Now you can do all of your shopping on the Internet and find enough information that you do not even need to go to the library anymore. Although it is wonderful, it can also cause problems because any ridiculous person can add information to the Internet for thousands of people to see.

Some of our devotees spend a good deal of time on the Internet now and they should be careful because some people do nothing but vomit on the Internet. Many years ago, someone put rumors on the Internet about me. They said that I had fallen down with two women in Alachua, was wearing white, and was trying to decide which of the two women to marry—unbelievable. The GBC had to ask me and another *sannyasi* to write a statement that we had not married. The *rtviks* created this whole idea that some of the *sannyasis* had married. It became such a rumor that people were accepting it. Some people just want to immerse themselves in nonsense or have failed in their own lives so they want to see others fail. We have to be very careful.

I hope that our devotees in our projects try to honor all the *asramas* in a genuine sense but at the same time remain fixed in their own *asramas*. Those who are ready to live as *brahmacaris* should remain *brahmacari* and those who are married should honor their marriage nicely by taking care of their devotional life as well as of their material responsibilities. If we do not take care of all of these aspects, we will become very disgruntled and stagnated in many ways. We will feel depressed if we cannot maintain a sense of devotion in our own life and within the community. Then when your daughter reaches sixteen and runs off in a miniskirt to meet some biker, you will wonder what happened. She will say, "Haribol Mother. I am on my way to Las Vegas and I got a really fun job at the casino. I'll see you for Janmastami. I found a really nice man who is thirty-five years old and very rich." You will wonder how your daughter ended up in this situation. Don't think that it can't happen to you. It has happened to so many others. If we do not have a sufficiently spiritual environment, the child will see this as something cynical and act differently, almost out of spite. We should not put ourselves and our children in that situation. We all know that some of our children are trying to sue the movement because they are angry or disturbed. We cannot talk them out of their feelings but we have to act in a way that shows them how Krishna consciousness works.

The First Shower of Nectar

Srila Visvanatha Cakravarti Thakura's first presentation in *The Bhakti Trilogy: Delineations on the Esoterics of Pure Devotion* is called the *Madhurya-Kadambini*. The word *kadambini* means a long bank of clouds that are showering *madhurya*, the sweetness of devotion. These clouds manifest over the environment to shower the *madhurya* and extinguish the blazing forest fire of material attraction and attachments. The rain cloud drops torrents of rain in order to extinguish the forest fire of material consciousness. The material senses have ignited the whole body and mind with fire. Consequently, the living entity's material existence in this world is on fire due to the agitated senses that are constantly demanding satisfaction. We are in material bodies, burning up due to sense gratification. Spiritual ecstasy, the *bhava* and *prema*, totally extinguish the fire and inaugurate a new age, which is actually the original experience.

This first chapter is called *The First Shower of Nectar*. *Srimad-Bhagavatam* 10.43.17 states that the wrestlers, the men of Mathura and the women all saw Krishna in different ways. Srila Visvanatha Cakravarti Thakura emphasizes this statement in order to clarify "that the gradual development of spiritual joy depends entirely on *rasa* and the degree of its intimacy. Therefore *rasa* is the singular support of spiritual happiness and bliss" (*Bhakti Trilogy*, 3). Even in our neophyte stage, we may have an attraction to a certain Deity, to certain literatures, to specific personalities and even to certain situations that stimulate us more than others. Some devotees feel surcharged after reading the *Mahabharata* because it gives them a great sense of commitment, a sense of identity and a sense of value. Other devotees may find more solace in the *Bhagavad-gita*, *Caitanya-caritamrta*, or *The Nectar of Devotion*. Hopefully some devotees will find solace in all of these literatures. These attractions can also relate to the actual eternal position of the soul, which is present and knows its ultimate alignment with Krishna. However, the mind and intelligence may be in denial or may even attempt to interfere. Many of these great *acaryas* who we often read about have such special ultimate relationships with Krishna that their services, commissions or writings directly correlate to their eternal mellow of exchange, service and love in the spiritual world.

The Cause of Bhakti

The Lord and *suddha-bhakti* are self-manifest and independent. It may confuse us to try to pinpoint the cause of *bhakti*. How is it controlled? How is it given up? How is it experienced?

The First Shower of Nectar

> *"As the Supreme Lord independently appears to the jivas by His own sweet will, so Bhakti-devi is also self-manifest and fully independent, appearing in any place of her choice. (There is no difference between sakti, or energy, and the energetic principle; hence, devotional service, or bhakti, is non-different from the Lord in all respects.)"*
>
> *Bhakti Trilogy, 3*

Therefore, *Srimad-Bhagavatam* 1.2.6 states:

> *"The supreme occupation (dharma) for all humanity is that by which men can attain to loving devotional service unto the transcendent Lord. Such devotional service must be unmotivated and uninterrupted to completely satisfy the self."*

Srila Visvanatha Cakravarti Thakura explains that loving devotion "must be without any motive for personal gain. This establishes that *bhakti* is unfettered by causes or conditions" (*Bhakti Trilogy*, 4). No material obstacle exists that can ultimately check *bhakti*. Although we can procrastinate or not honor Bhakti-devi, her appearance does not depend on any material, conditional situation.

The major concern is how the Lord bestows His

mercy and pure *bhakti*. Does Krishna practice favoritism by sometimes bestowing *bhakti* and at other times withholding it? Does He bestow it on certain planets or in certain universes while withholding it from other places? Does He bestow the *bhakti* according to how we ingratiate Him? Actually, none of these factors play a role. The various Vedic scriptures mention certain factors to help us determine which activities or mindsets are responsible for the *bhakti*. *Srimad-Bhagavatam* 11.20.8 states:

> *yadrcchaya mat-kathadau*
> *jata-sraddhas tu yah puman*
> *na nirvinno nati-sakto*
> *bhakti-yogo 'sya siddhi-dah*

> *"Bhakti has been described by the word yadrcchaya, or 'own volition'... For example, is this fortune because of pious activities? or misfortune because of impious acts? or simply a lack of good actions? If we accept that good fortune as a result of pious activities creates bhakti, then it makes bhakti dependent upon, and subservient to, pious activities."*
>
> Bhakti Trilogy, 4

It is not some type of business arrangement that can be controlled by people's actions or by a type of reciprocity that deals with the externals. *Bhakti*

The First Shower of Nectar

does not manifest from imperfection or impiousness, because something perfect cannot come from something imperfect. Furthermore, are the blessings based on action? Not exactly, because we see that different actions can produce different types of ultimate outcomes. "It is certain that after much probing and speculation a single irrefutable cause will not be established" (*Bhakti Trilogy*, 4).

> "Just as the Lord's mercy is known to be causeless, so His devotees who possess the same qualities as the Lord also shower their causeless mercy. Hence, when we declare that the devotee's causeless mercy is the reason which inspires bhakti, but that bhakti is not being equally distributed, naturally this will be criticized as partiality."
>
> *Bhakti Trilogy*, 5

In other words, Krishna is called *bhakta-vatsalya* which means that He seems to give special recognition to His *bhaktas*. He gives this special recognition although He does not really have favorites. Actually, the *bhaktas* are receiving more because they are responding more and are more receptive. Due to their receptivity, there is a different endowment upon them.

The *Srimad-Bhagavatam* 11.2.46 states:

> "An intermediate or second-class devotee, called madhyama-adhikari, offers his love to the Supreme Personality of Godhead, is a sincere friend to all the devotees of the Lord, shows mercy to ignorant people who are innocent and disregards those who are envious of the Supreme Personality of Godhead."

In other words, they make a distinction between those who are favorably serving the Lord in contrast to those who are envious of the Lord. Consequently, the devotee relates to each person differently. Then one may wonder if Krishna also bestows His mercy based on these distinctions.

> "These characteristics clearly indicate that the madhyama-adhikari devotee does not distribute his mercy equally to everyone. The truth is that the Supreme Lord is subservient to His devotee's wishes; therefore, He emulates His devotee in disbursing mercy."
>
> Bhakti Trilogy, 5

Consequently, if these are the actions of the devotee and Krishna is a servant of His devotees, Krishna must also make the distinction because He is bound to His devotees. Since the Supreme Lord is subservient to His devotees' wishes, He emulates His devotee in the distribution of the mercy.

> *"Based on this fact it is easy to see that if the madhyama devotee is merciful to someone, the Lord automatically showers His mercy on that recipient. This conclusion is sound in all respects. The single cause that attracts the mercy of the Lord is the bhakti, which permanently resides in the pure devotee's heart. In other words, Krishna's mercy will not be invoked without that bhakti within the heart of His devotee, which attracts His mercy to appear in the first place. Therefore, because bhakti is completely independent, even from previous piety and good fortune, it is undisputedly confirmed that bhakti is self-manifest. As mentioned earlier, devotion is the only cause of devotion; Bhakti-devi does not require any cause or reason to appear other than her own sweet will."*
>
> *Bhakti Trilogy, 5*

She is eternally manifest in the heart of everyone but her manifestation is much more pronounced in the heart of the pure devotee. Therefore *bhakti* is made available by the mercy of the pure devotees who themselves have that *bhakti* sacredly locked up in their hearts.

Krishna allows Himself to be bound by the love of His devotees. According to this reciprocity, the devotee is all for the Lord and He is all for the devotees, even to the point of fulfilling the wishes of His unadulterated devotee. Bhakti-devi comes out at this point and not as a result of other conditions. Knowledge is a prerequisite but will not give us *bhakti*. *Yajnas*, austerities, *bhajanas*, *kirtanas*, the nine-fold process, or the four rules will not fully lead to pure devotion. They only help us become candidates to receive. Again, the *Srimad-Bhagavatam* 11.12.9 explains:

yam na yogena sankhyena
dana-vrata-tapo-'dhvaraih
vyakhya-svadhyaya-sannyasaih
prapnuyad yatnavan api

"That devotional service cannot be obtained even by diligently cultivating yoga, empirical and deductive knowledge, performing charity, fasting, penances, sacrifices, studying and analyzing the Vedas, renunciation, etc."

If even these practices cannot give pure devotion, the goal may seem impossible. However, we understand that devotion is the property of Krishna and the pure devotees of the Lord.

Krishna Submits to His Devotees

> "Here, one may present a counter argument, saying that devotees are always under the Lord's control, therefore how can the devotee's mercy appear first, independently, and not as a successor to the Lord's causeless compassion? Krishna Himself provides the solution to this problem by openly declaring that He is voluntarily subservient to His pure devotees."
>
> Bhakti Trilogy, 6

Krishna is so powerful, merciful and compassionate that He allows Himself to be controlled and He allows His power to come under the wishes and jurisdiction of His pure devotee. This is a sign of great power. Someone may have great strength, power and expertise but they can only function as the controlling element. However, when they put themselves at the mercy of others, they cannot control in the same way. Krishna's power is so consistent that He does not have to be served as the *Isvara*. As a matter of fact, He does not even prefer to be honored in this way. He does not have to be understood or known as the Supreme Autocrat for His power to manifest and dominate over all. He does not have to worry about losing His grip simply because people do not recognize His position as the ultimate controller and maintainer. It is just the opposite. Krishna experiences greater happiness when the cowherd boys sometimes defeat Him, jump on His back or demand that He carries them. He still shows His own power when He lifts Govardhana Hill or defeats the various demons. However, He is more satisfied when the power comes through His devotees and people honor the power that comes through them. Consequently He supports the wishes of His pure devotees.

Devotees are Spiritual Warriors

This is one of the exalted aspects of Krishna consciousness and the reason for our constant emphasis on Krishna's representatives. They are so eager to serve the devotees; therefore, we are even more eager to serve them. This reciprocation cannot be easily understood by the non-devotees and may confuse people at times. For instance, we recently honored Srila Prabhupada's disappearance day, which has helped the devotees all around the world to more intensely reflect upon him. I have been receiving amazing e-mails and phone calls from some godbrothers who are trying to find ways to revitalize their Krishna consciousness. These special appearance and disappearance days often cause us to reflect more on our promises and to scrutinize our consistency in following the promises made before the founder-*acarya*, the assembly of devotees, the Deities and to ourselves. These times often help us refocus and recommit ourselves. In

The First Shower of Nectar

some of these phone calls and letters, the devotees have described how they are trying to continue their offering to Srila Prabhupada and are working to recapture the pioneering spirit of their earlier years. As we grow older, we increasingly realize that we do not want to retire, but we want to maintain the spirit that Srila Prabhupada had during his last days while transmitting the message of the *Bhagavatam* from his bed. He continued to share his own ecstasies and love due to his commitment to his *guru* and to the other great *acaryas*. He gave this offering in a special package that we can continue to read and appreciate now.

Those of us who follow that spirit of Prabhupada understand that we are to die on the battlefield. Each individual must choose their own battlefield, but we must leave our bodies in battle. So we find ways to continually engage our bodies and minds in devotional service. When Prabhupada's body could no longer remain active, he still continued to use his mind in service. This is the umbrella that we are all under. Our founder-*acarya* showed us by his own example how to glorify the Lord despite the external circumstances. Despite the challenges within the environment or within ourselves, we can always find some way to use any energy or facility to create an offering for *guru* and Krishna. Srila Prabhupada had stopped eating, sleeping and had certainly stopped mating and defending. He did not even have the physical strength to hold the microphone, but with his little breath, he continued to speak and give. His voice was barely audible but he continued to speak into the microphone. This is definitely a sign to all of us for generations to come. There is never a time or a situation in which we cannot somehow glorify Krishna. As long as we have some breath or mental reflection, we can always find a way to offer it back. Whatever we may have, we find some way to give it to *guru* and Krishna. As we honor Srila Prabhupada's disappearance around the world, hopefully we have reflected more deeply on how Srila Prabhupada gave so extensively and how we also want to give in such ways.

Everything Depends on Bhakti

> *"Hence the Srimad-Bhagavatam 11.20.32-33 states, 'Everything that can be achieved by fruitive activities, penance, knowledge, detachment, mystic yoga, charity, religious duties, and all other means of perfecting life is easily achieved by devotees through loving service to Me.'"*
>
> *Bhakti Trilogy, 9*

Again we see that everything ultimately happens successfully due to the *bhakti*. Even *jnana*, *karma*, and *yoga* depend on the element of *bhakti*. Therefore *bhakti* produces *bhakti* and everything comes back to *bhakti*.

Srila Visvanatha Cakravarti Thakura himself

deeply honors the offerings of Srila Jiva Goswami and helps to clarify the actual *Vaisnava siddhanta*. There have always been and always will be times of obfuscation and confusion about the proper duty of a *Vaisnava*, but Krishna wonderfully arranges for special agents to appear and make this wonderful knowledge available. It is available for us to embrace and to accept as an integral part of present day *bhakti* on this planet. The *Prabhupada Lilamrta*, the *Abhay Charan* video series, the books and the tapes all give a powerful presentation of this modern day offering to the world. As we carefully scrutinize this offering, we will understand that Lord Caitanya is personally making it happen, often in spite of our shortcomings. Krishna constantly uses His agents. Although He can do everything Himself, He desires to show His power by the way in which He uses others. For instance, Srila Prabhupada often spoke before large crowds of people, but instead of speaking himself, he would sometimes call on one of his disciples to speak. Not only would he call on the men but he would also call on the women. The expertise of Prabhupada's disciples would show his power even more. The power, love and effectiveness of his mission could be even more appreciated through many of these effects.

Effort vs. Mercy

Our last topic in this section involves the issue of effort versus mercy. Mercy must be present, but mercy also relates to effort. As we previously mentioned, *bhakti* does not depend on piety, favoritism, certain deeds, etc. It is not under the control of any of these factors. We can also examine mercy in this way in order to understand how it is given. If mercy is causeless, do we just wait for it to happen? If it depends on action, can we call it causeless? Then it might appear to be *karma-kanda* in which one performs certain actions to obtain certain reactions. This might lead to the question asked in Krishna's discussion with Nanda Maharaja. Krishna says to Nanda Maharaja that there is no need to worship the demigods since everything simply goes on by the law of *karma*. By this philosophy, worship of the demigods or God is irrelevant if one simply experiences reactions based on *karma*. What then is the need of worshipping Krishna if everything just depends on these laws? If we just engage in certain *yajnas* or *pujas* and receive certain types of results, what is the need for all this personal service to the Deity, to *guru*, to *sadhu*, etc.?

We must always act as if the ultimate result depends on ourselves. We do our best in any endeavor, but at the same time we must recognize that we are not the ultimate controllers. However, we act in the spirit that the results do depend on us. For this reason, certain *rasas* such as *vatsalya-rasa* are so powerful, even more than *sakhya-rasa*. In *vatsalya-rasa*, one thinks that Krishna needs service. We see Him as a young child; therefore, He is so much in need that His existence depends upon how we care for Him. For these reasons, this *rasa* is

The First Shower of Nectar

even more dynamic than *sakhya-rasa*. We should act with commitment, dedication, absorption, intensity and attentiveness as if the results depend on our actions, while simultaneously realizing that Krishna is the ultimate controller. Therefore, we do our best without claiming ultimate proprietorship.

We appreciate that the effort begins to position us for the mercy. If we engage in certain actions and obtain certain results, how do we avoid accepting the results as our own, and how do we avoid false ego and pride when we understand that it is our duty to have pride? How can we honor Krishna, Prabhupada and the great *Vaisnava acaryas* if we do not have pride in them? How can we honor the *Bhagavad-gita, Srimad-Bhagavatam*, or *Caitanya-caritamrta* if we do not have intense pride in what they represent and give us? However, this same pride can lead to our downfall and keep us in the material world. This is the nature of all the higher aspects of *bhakti*. Philosophy refers to this as diunital because of a seeming opposition or contradiction, but all higher things at first appear contradictory. When we study them closer, they give us different flavors and mellows that help us to understand the various aspects in a more holistic way. We should have intense pride, otherwise we will be embarrassed or intimidated, we will not take full advantage of the opportunities available, or we will think of this process as another religion, another philosophy or just another book. It will seem acceptable to let everyone do what they want and honor what they choose in order to help them feel good. However, this is not what the great *acaryas* have given us. They have tremendous humility, but at the same time, tremendous pride. Srila Rupa Goswami expresses this mood in his *asa-bandha* prayer. He feels that he does not have this kind of achievement, love of God or even love for the engagements that help one to develop love. However, he has this complete and unwavering conviction that he will receive the mercy of the Lord and pride in his appreciation of Krishna's causeless mercy. He understands the availability of the causeless mercy; therefore, he will align himself to be able to receive that mercy. We should not have pride in our own achievements, but as we execute our work and as we do achieve, we have pride and respect for Krishna who comes through. We should also have pride and respect for what Krishna's agents have arranged. We should put forth great effort with determination and work intensely as if it depends on us but, at the same time, we offer the results to the Lord.

This is the great power of *bhakti* and the way in which *bhakti* works. For example, someone may be stuck in a well and unable to escape, but if someone throws a rope into the well, the person can grab on tightly in order to climb out. The person who escaped from the well may begin to think that they obtained their freedom simply as a result of their own abilities and efforts. Of course, effort was necessary to grab the rope but mercy was most dominant. The mercy came from the person who threw the rope and the imprisoned individual gained freedom due to this mercy. However, the person did not obtain freedom solely due to mercy, because although the mercy was delivered, the person had to put forth the effort and grab hold of the rope. The effort combined with the mercy produces the success and produces the achievement. Krishna and His agents give us the mercy, but we must put forth the effort and endeavor to connect with that mercy. This is the causeless position. It is causeless and not based on favoritism.

We Must Make Ourselves Available

The Lord is *bhakta-vatsalya*, which means that we may receive more than another individual according to the extent that we make ourselves available to receive the mercy. We must grab the rope and hold on while carefully giving honor to the Lord's mercy. Otherwise, we may succeed in grabbing the rope initially, but if we accept ourselves as the achiever, the next opportunity will result in failure or the mercy will pass us by. Srila Prabhupada has extended the rope that previous *acaryas* have extended again and again. Should we just analyze the rope without grabbing hold? Should we simply throw it back, considering that the endeavor is too difficult? Should we become overly distracted and forget about the chance to rise above? Many obstacles can interfere if we do not understand the need for effort and also the position of mercy. One may feel completely defeated while stuck in such a debilitating situation and just die. However, the mercy always exists, and since it is causeless, it does not come as a result of knowledge, austerity, *jnana*, etc. We cannot simply chant a mantra to invoke the mercy. Nevertheless, the mercy is available and causeless, but when it reaches us, what is the quality of our effort and how do we honor it so that it continually manifests in our lives? If we do not properly honor the mercy when it comes periodically, it will seem to stop coming because Krishna promises that, as we surrender, He rewards us accordingly. He tells us through Srila Visvanatha Cakravarti that the mercy is locked up in the heart of His devotees and that Krishna purposely enjoys letting His power manifest through His agents even more than through Himself. Therefore, if there is not healthy and proper *sadhu-sanga*, the mercy will not emerge so easily. If we focus too much on our own abilities, we will miss the mercy. If we fail to appreciate the power of mercy and do not put forth the necessary effort, we will expect the mercy to simply descend upon us and we will be disappointed. The proper mindset involves taking advantage of the rope through effort while offering proper appreciation to the carriers of the mercy who extend the rope.

Questions & Answers
Question: You mentioned that some people might have an attraction to certain Deities or books. Does this always signify some deeper connection or could it simply be a shallow attachment due to previous

The First Shower of Nectar

material conditionings that may change after a period of time?

Answer: It could be all of this and more, or it could be based on the ego. Someone might say, "I do not read *Bhagavad-gita* since it is for neophytes. I only want to read some of the very sweet pastimes of Krishna in Vrndavana." Someone might think, "Chant rounds and follow regulated activities? No, this is for neophytes. I simply want to express my innermost love of Krishna as He expresses it to me." However, it may also just be an artificial shadow of a certain mellow, which can change. Someone in their current state of evolution in Krishna consciousness may really admire the position of the cowherd boys who wrestle and play with Krishna. However, as their consciousness unfolds, they may distinctly find that their ultimate association or *rasa* is in the mood of *madhurya*. The material personality that lacks real identity and surrender may want to wrestle with Krishna in order to beat Him; therefore, they reflect in this mood. It is not necessarily coming from their real position or their original *svarupa*. However, there are instances in which these feelings actually come from this position.

Question: It seems, like the old adage, that whom you know is more important than what you do. How would you respond to this?

Answer: There is truth to this statement, because

our relationship with the representatives or systems will definitely have a more significant effect on us. You may know and align yourself with someone who teaches impersonalism or *karma-kanda*, which means that they have a connection with such. However, whom we meet and connect with also depends on credits and effort from previous lifetimes and credits and effort in the present life along with mercy. Many people received the mercy to know Srila Prabhupada through previous credits and ultimately through mercy. Then the question arises of how you know him. Some people knew him in the early days but never took initiation, which means that they knew him in a certain way. Some people who knew him took initiation, but as soon as he left the planet, they also left the movement. So, the question is, "Who do you know and how do you know them?"

Question: When you discussed pride, you talked about having pride in Srila Prabhupada or in *sastra*, but you also warned us about pride as a potential cause for fall down. Could we clarify pride by stating that devotees do not have pride in themselves but pride in *guru* or in *sastra* which actually means dovetailing pride in Krishna consciousness?

Answer: It means that one has genuine pride and appreciation in our wonderful scriptures and pride in Krishna's arrangement to give us shelter under our great founder-*acarya* Srila Prabhupada. The devotee has genuine pride in Krishna's wonderful pastimes, not just in His aspect of *aisvarya* or as the great controller, but also through these many wonderful expressions and exchanges. We ask all the devotees to intensify their basic mood of appreciation. We are trying to focus more, which means being genuinely happy, stimulated, motivated and proud of the ability to engage in the process of devotion. It does not mean being proud of our individual accomplishments that simply stem from our own intelligence. In that case, the false ego would capture us and we would see ourselves as the controllers and proprietors. However, if we do not have pride, we will lack enthusiasm, commitment, firm faith and determination. People who minimize the power of this *Vaisnava siddhanta* will never catch up with it sufficiently. They will think, "I will engage in some Krishna consciousness now and a little *hatha-yoga* or *kriya-yoga* later. I will accept one *guru* now but another *guru* later." Some people think in this way, viewing Krishna consciousness as another one of the smorgasbord of activities. They might also think, "In my youth, I really needed that practice but now that I am a mature adult, I no longer need this idea of a personal God and the rules and regulations." We do not want to be in denial by seeing ourselves as responsible or in denial of the power of that love.

Question: We know that mercy can come in a very positive way or in seemingly adverse ways. We also know that a devotee is free of *karma* after taking initiation but the fan continues to run. How do we differentiate the adversities that happen to us on the path of devotional service? Is it mercy or is it *karmic* reaction? Should we have a positive outlook or realistically accept such reactions as a result of our past activities?

Answer: This can relate to the idea of the fan. Sometimes the fan moves very powerfully, and although you may turn off the power, it is still powerful. It still has some momentum. Although there may be some alteration from the initiation, we may carry so much other stuff that the same patterns cause the fan to again move very fast. In a similar mood, the devotee accepts any adversity as their own fault, thinking that they deserve even more. At the same time, they honor the fact that, since Krishna does not make any mistakes, He has a good reason for allowing such adversities to be a part of our field of activities. This is the point at which we need humility, great appreciation and the recognition of Krishna as our well-wisher. Otherwise, if we dive into the adverse conditions too deeply, it means that later we will start blaming Krishna, since He ultimately controls everything. We realize that Krishna honors our free will, allowing us to engage in activities and to receive reciprocation accordingly. Therefore, we accept any difficulty as our fault. We blame ourselves, thinking that we deserve worse, but simultaneously we endeavor to receive Krishna's mercy through our effort. Otherwise, people run away from God or from

The First Shower of Nectar

the spiritual path because they think the spiritual path means no difficulties. Actually, nothing is more difficult than following a spiritual path. To be on a spiritual path means being in the material world and in a material body while saying, "To hell with all of that!" It means not making the material a priority even though the material environment revolves around material priorities. How can we expect peace when we are moving directly against the grain? Sometimes ignorance produces more of a sense of peace than dealing with the reality and developing knowledge and wisdom. The cheaters view religion in this way, in relation to peace, because to a certain extent they are still trying to use God and religion as a means to arrange for their material desires and remove interferences. Consequently, they look for peace instead of service and ultimate association. On the other hand, we want ultimate association and service; therefore, the spiritual path becomes difficult while we move all the material attachments and illusions to the side. As we take to spiritual life, we should expect to do serious work on ourselves. We have to look closer at what *bhakti* is, how *bhakti* comes, and how to properly honor it. Furthermore, we should recognize the presence of the mercy, but simultaneously put forth effort.

The Second Shower of Nectar

The Science of Faith

We are examining the various intricacies of coming to devotional service and executing devotional service along with the esoteric ways that Bhakti-devi relates to the living entity. We will now discuss the *Second Shower of Nectar*. We know the importance of *sraddha* or faith when it comes to engaging in devotional service. At times people may feel shy or intimidated by the whole idea of faith, declaring that the entire process of religiosity is just a matter of blind faith. They claim that religion itself is just "hype" because nobody really discovers the truth until after death. Or they see religion as a way to appease people with artificial aspirations about a higher reality. We do not accept this as real religion. For some people, religion may be just a matter of axioms, dogmas, rituals and hypocrisy but this is not really religion. When we closely examine real religion and knowledge, we see that real knowledge means understanding the necessity of engaging in devotional service. The more knowledge we have, *budha bhava-samanvitah*, the more we dedicate ourselves to Krishna.

When there is genuine knowledge and understanding, there is corresponding attachment and absorption. We do not feel shy about faith, but the important factor is how we repose the faith. We understand that everything involves faith, even in certain secular situations, and we see that the quality of our faith will lead to certain types of alignments. When some people experience distress, their faith brings them to Krishna. When other people undergo distress, their faith leads them to vigorously engage in sense gratification. We may have had some basic faith in Krishna, but due to some challenge or problem in our lives, we may actually start turning against Krishna or lose enthusiasm to participate in practically all devotional activities. Another person may also have problems but they just involve themselves more deeply in the devotional process. Each case relates to the quality of faith, which relates to the quality of consciousness. So Bhakti-devi notices and responds to the quality of faith in relationship to consciousness.

Types of Bhakti

> *"Now we shall discuss bhakti and the symptoms of bhakti. There are two kinds of bhakti: sraddha (devotional service performed with faith) and misra (mixed devotional service)."*
>
> *Bhakti Trilogy, 14*

The Second Shower of Nectar

Mixed devotional service manifests in different ways. It is devotional service with some extra contamination that does not belong. For instance, maybe you are trying to cook a meal, but because you are distracted, you add salt instead of sugar.

Visvanatha Cakravarti first discusses *misra*, which includes *karma-misra-bhakti*, *jnana-misra-bhakti*, and *yoga-misra-bhakti*. *Karma-misra-bhakti* includes *bhakti* but it is mixed with fruitive moods and desires. *Jnana-misra-bhakti* also involves *bhakti* along with extensive mental speculation. Instead of trying to serve, to know and to experience, we are more in the mood of trying to be a *pandita* without following. One still deals with the activities and discussions of *bhakti* but *bhakti* does not come forward so strongly because it is mixed. One engaged in *yoga-misra-bhakti* is mostly interested in *siddhic* powers and mysticism. The link is there but it is contaminated.

> *"Bhakti-devi is the inspiration for all activities favorable to the process of surrender to the Supreme Lord. Like the touchstone, Bhakti-devi gradually converts the iron of material sense perception to the gold of spiritual understanding merely by the power of her association."*
>
> *Bhakti Trilogy, 14*

Just as a touchstone turns ordinary metal into

gold, *bhakti* combined with *yoga, jnana* and *karma* will lead to some success. However, as the *bhakti* increases more and more, it will all turn into *suddha-bhakti*.

> "From this creeper of devotion burgeons two fresh leaves both representing sadhana-bhakti, or regulated devotional service. The first leaf is called klesaghni (destroyer of distresses), and the second leaf is known as subhada (bestower of good fortune). (These two leaves may also be described as vaidhi-bhakti, regulated devotional service, and raga-bhakti, spontaneous devotional service. Their difference of mood depends entirely on the practitioner's level of realization). The soft inner core of these two leaves represents the devotee's mood of constant hankering for a loving relationship with the Lord and His eternal associates. When he attains this loving relationship, the devotee feels that he belongs to the beloved Lord and His associates. This elevated stage is known as raga-bhakti, or spontaneous love."
>
> Bhakti Trilogy, 14

This occurs when the devotee has intense *laulya*

or intense hankering and deeply wants to regain his or her original consciousness. Bhakti-devi takes notice of this desire and responds according to the degree of faith and determination. However, it is not only based on these factors but also on the nine-fold process and the rituals that set the stage. The real influx of *bhakti* is causeless, but it exists in relationship to the carriers of *bhakti*. *Bhakti* does not fully surface unless it comes through the carriers of *bhakti*. In this sense, it depends on whom you know and on what you know. They all relate, because whom you know and what you know are also related to Bhakti-devi's knowledge of your desires, intentions and previous credits. Of course, the mercy is most important. We examined the equal importance of mercy and effort previously.

Causes of Distress

The next section examines the causes of distress. There are specific causes of anxieties or problems and corresponding means to neutralize them. If we understand some of these negative causes of mixed devotion, we can see the enemy in order to avoid it and minimize its growth. Srila Visvanatha Cakravarti Thakura gives us a list of enemies that cause distress so that when we find ourselves in this type of mentality, we can understand the cause of our predicament. A real devotee's distress only emerges due to their desire to serve Krishna better and their feelings of sorrow for the suffering people who are avoiding Krishna. There is really no other reason to feel distress. Any other reason is superfluous.

Lack of True Knowledge

The first cause of distress is nescience or lack of knowledge. The opposite—proper knowledge and understanding—casts out our distress. He mentions that certain feelings such us unhappiness, remorsefulness or different types of *maya* chase Bhakti-devi away. In the presence of Bhakti-devi there is firm faith, enthusiasm and determination.

False Ego

The next cause is *ahankara* or false ego. If we feel some distress, we should look to see what is dominating our consciousness. Is it nescience, or am I taking too much mental shelter of the illusion? Am I blocking my mind and intelligence from full absorption in the reflections of transcendence? On the cover of *Back to Godhead* it says, "Godhead is light. Nescience is darkness. Where there is Godhead there is no nescience." In the presence of light, the darkness must go. This darkness is clouding our consciousness. When we pull away the nescience, we will no longer experience distress. If we take away the false ego, we will have the genuine, divine ego.

We all have our own propensities and idiosyncratic tendencies. These proclivities are real because the soul itself is full of activities and full of expression. However, now that the false ego and intelligence accept the senses and the mind as their bosses, there are problems. We need to accelerate our divine ego since we are spiritual beings undergoing a material experience, rather than material beings trying to have a spiritual experience. If we act according to our own plan and then try to relate it to Krishna, the ego will cause us to stumble in different ways and we will feel distress. We should try to think of how to bring about the greatest spiritual effect and position ourselves to assist either directly or indirectly. Everything that deals with *misra,* or mixed *bhakti,* brings pain and distress. We do not want to pass months, years, or even lifetimes in anxiety. We all experience anxiety from time to time, and it is very hellish. Anger, sadness and depression are very hellish. We almost become like monsters and begin thinking, "I am angry. Don't even look at me. Do not say anything to me. I am a victim. Do not smile at me. Cry with me. Cry harder than me so that I will not feel so victimized. Maybe I will see that you are also a victim. We can have a victim party or a pity party." These mindsets are very intense and lead us into a dark well without any light for us. We just end up bathing in ignorance, nescience or the false ego. Much of the false ego is centered on selfishness. The more that we just think of ourselves, the more we are supporting or fueling the fire of false ego. Gradually we will begin to feel gloomy and our enthusiasm will burn away, along with our devotional credits.

Material Attachments

Material attachments are the third cause of distress because all material objects are actually temporary. An eternal being who makes the material a priority will definitely feel miserable. Simply looking at food in a window cannot satisfy a hungry person. Someone may bring a large plate of artificial fruits and vegetables, but you cannot enjoy it. You may wonder, "What is happening. I still feel weak and hungry. It looks so beautiful but it is not nourishing." When people put excessive energy into the enjoyment of material attachments, they will feel great distress because these material pleasures do not give real stimulation.

Envy

Srila Visvanatha Cakravarti next explains envy. A devotee feels the happiness of others as well as their distress. They are to be selfless and compassionate. A devotee is sad that he is not serving better and sad due to the distress of another. In this way, devotees do not envy because they feel happiness when others are happy. There is no question of envy. Since they lack this ego, they do not think, "I deserve this benediction. I should have this material position. I am much better than that person." This mindset of self-centeredness will draw envy. Ironically, the more people put their energy into thinking about themselves, the more they suffer. If you have prepared a nice meal but continue to add improper ingredients, what happens? You will not make a better preparation. If you try to fix the sweet rice by adding salt, it will not taste better. The more salt you add, the worse it will taste.

Visvanatha Cakravarti explains that these

contaminations chase away Bhakti-devi and lead to *misra-bhakti*. He tries to help us understand how the enemy looks and how it manifests so that we can identify it and eliminate the cause of distress. If these sources of distress are not eliminated, we will feel more and more suffering. We all need to look at ourselves from time to time and think, "Am I actually happy in devotional service? Am I excited? Am I anticipating greater and greater chances to unfold on all different levels?" Or, do we look at ourselves and think, "I feel depressed, sad, angry, envious, jealous and faithless." We have to decide if we are going to weed out these problems or if we are just going to add more of the same negativity that created the difficulty in the first place. If we intensify our faithlessness, nescience, false ego and material attachments, we will just become stuck. We occasionally see this manifest in our own lives. We may face a difficult situation and turn to unhealthy activities. When some people are bewildered in their devotional service, they turn again to cigarettes, prostitutes or intoxications. Instead of intensifying their consciousness and endeavoring to eliminate the distress, *maya* will influence them to engage in activities that will cause more distress. What makes the difference? The difference is *sraddha*, mercy, and *sukrti*. Our previous credits determine how we will respond. So Srila Visvanatha Cakravarti encourages us to look closer at nescience, false ego, material attachments and envy.

Mundane Engagements

The last of the five is mundane engrossment or mundane engagements. This is similar to attachments but of an even lower nature. Attachments can be subtle or gross, but this specifically refers to the absorption in the gross attachments. We cannot cheat Krishna—this should be obvious. We cannot think of Krishna as dull, insensitive or impersonal and engage in all types of crazy activities while still expecting Bhakti-devi to bless us and reciprocate with us. She does not want to come to an environment filled with the associates of *maya* just as a royal person has no desire to enter a degraded place. A clean and brahminical person would feel uncomfortable in an environment filled with *prajalpa* and sinful activities. Even the entities from the higher planets do not want to come into environments filled with the modes of passion and ignorance. So *bhakti* draws *bhakti*. If we try to pursue a devotional lifestyle but simultaneously engage in all this other nonsense, we will send a signal to Bhakti-devi that we really do not want her. Unfortunately, as we chase away the *bhakti*, we bring in more nescience, pain, distress and sadness.

Recently I went on a tour of France, Switzerland, Sweden, Austria, Italy and a few other countries and found it painful to see the number of *Vaisnavas* feeling miserable. Why? Prabhupada did not cheat us; therefore, we must be cheating. The devotees were not experiencing distress due to the pain that they saw in others; their sadness revolved around

The Second Shower of Nectar

"I" and "mine." Prabhupada did not create a society for us to come together to mutually suffer while we think about transcendence. Nobody wants to suffer or be unnecessarily surrounded with suffering.

Although someone may have wealth, if they are filthy, a brahminical person will not desire their company. There is no reason for such filth. There is a difference between those who are poor and those who are just negligent. In the villages, the people may be simple and poor but they are often very clean and have some spunk about life because they value what they do have. I have seen small villages in India, Africa and Latin America where people rise early every morning, clean their entire areas, and even take several baths a day. There are many people in "modern" society today who do not bathe every day. Although we consider a daily bath as a natural part of the day, the majority of people on this planet do not bathe every day. If you stand at a rest stop for 5 or 10 minutes, you will see that most people do not even wash their hands after using the toilet. We see that even the aristocratic class and royalty of the past did not bathe regularly. It is for this reason that French perfume is so powerful. In ancient times people dressed very effulgently but often did not bathe; therefore, there was a need for powerful perfume. There are huge castles with big rooms filled with tremendous splendor but no bathrooms. The aristocratic class in Europe often did not have bathrooms in those days. In these huge castles, they would just go into a room and use buckets.

They were sophisticated animals. The rich Greeks and Romans also had gruesome habits. They would eat huge amounts of food and then vomit in silver or golden pans so that they could continue eating more. It was comparable to bulimia. They were not concerned about their weight but simply wanted to enjoy more and more.

The way we are living or are trying to live is quite different. When I was a child in school, we used to talk about the Saturday night bath. We would bathe once a week on Saturdays and some children even disliked that because they would have to stop playing to take the bath. Most people I knew just bathed by throwing some water on their face and using a small washcloth. And the lack of hygiene in college was unbelievable. The Ivy League University I attended was supposedly filled with intelligent individuals prepared to change the world, but most of them had a very low consciousness. My prep school was filled with super rich people who were also extremely degraded.

If you want to absorb yourself in hearing and thinking about Krishna but your associates simply engage in *prajalpa*, you should feel uncomfortable. However, if your consciousness contains envy, nescience and false ego, not only will you feel comfortable but you will look for people with a similar mentality. For this reason, many times when devotees fall, they associate with other fallen devotees in order to rationalize their own deviation. Since they know Krishna, they cannot get the knowledge out of their consciousness fully, but at the same time, they are not ready to give up this *misra-bhakti*. Then the tendency is to seek out environments that will help reinforce their nescience. In this way, they do not have to recognize the level of their nescience or endeavor to eradicate it. *Maya* uses all of these different tricks to reinforce the illusion.

Neutralizing the Causes of Distress

These five negative qualities cause the distress and, if we eliminate them, we will not experience such disturbances. A devotee should not experience any distress that does not result from compassion. If we are in distress, it means that we have to do our homework more seriously. We have to more genuinely and consciously follow the process.

After describing the causes of distress, Srila Visvanatha Cakravarti then examines the means to neutralize them. He gives four stages of sinful reactions that are a part of the distress. *Prarabdha* are sins that have already matured and that have produced certain types of results or problems in our lives. The second category is called *aprarabdha* or sins that have not yet matured. They have not caught up with us or begun to beat us yet. They are in the background, waiting for their chance to attack us and chastise us. *Kuta* is the stage before the seed. *Bija* is the seed stage. We understand the need to stop the sinful activities but we must also weed out the seed. Sometimes we stop the sinful activities but leave the seed. In this case, sufficient nourishment will cause the seed to sprout and later turn into sinful actions and thoughts. Farmers understand this science. First they plow up the ground and then plant. The *bija* is the stage before the actual seed is planted. Certain preparations are required and, once the seed is planted, you can add water and later harvest the result. Harvesting compares to the mature stage after the plant has grown and fructified. When the plant is still underground or unripe, it means that the seed has not yet matured. All of these stages of farming are analogous to the stages of sin. We have to check it and stop the plans for the sin. For example, when Lord Caitanya cleaned the Gundica temple, He cleaned the gross and the subtle. Then He even cleaned the outside. He not only looked closely at the gross and subtle but He also made arrangements to prevent these contaminations from reentering.

If we do not deal with the seed and the mentality that produces the weeds, the weeds will grow, gradually choking the creeper. It is much more difficult to root out the weed once it has grown strong and developed fully. It requires a greater endeavor to change once we situate our consciousness and senses in *maya*. It becomes very difficult because the contamination is now a part of our consciousness. When we fall, the deviation permeates our existence. It has a reverberating effect and so it takes more credits and adjustments to try to pick ourselves back up. Some people may never pick themselves up properly because the effects just

The Second Shower of Nectar

vibrate throughout their consciousness. For this reason, it is much better to avoid the deviation and not let the seed enter. However, if the seed is there, take it out. It is easier to remove a seed than to remove an entire plant along with its root. Then the initial weed may shed new seeds that will later cause more weeds to appear. These *anarthas* and *aparadhas* are bad enough, but the effects of these contaminations are even worse. The initial weed itself is a problem but unfortunately the one weed will surely produce more.

For example, the presence of one cockroach indicates the presence of many others who will certainly produce more. If it remains around, after a while the entire house will be infested with roaches. If you just let the problem continue, they will begin to jump out of cabinets, drawers or closets. Then you will wonder how the problem began in the first place. Maybe you had some food or garbage that sat for too many days. You created an environment that summoned the insects. If you prevent such an environment from developing, you will not have to deal with the consequences. If we do not have an alert consciousness, we will bring various contaminations into our minds and into our lives. Then we will undergo distress in trying to eliminate the problems that could have been avoided in the first place. Devotional service is simple, but becomes complicated when we are dishonest, lazy and take *maya* for granted. For this reason, the Lord's devotees have great compassion because they see how the living entities unnecessarily entangle themselves. The devotees feel compassion for a person engaged in sin because their improper activities will simply lead to negative reactions.

> *"Sins are abominable and they add only partly to man's material distress. The godly traits in man are his aversion toward the temporary, attraction for the divine that is connected to the Supreme, acceptance of that which is favorable to devotional service, mercy, forgiveness, truthfulness, simplicity, impartiality, patience, gravity, respectfulness, humility, and good fortune."*
> Bhakti Trilogy, 15

These qualities eliminate the weeds, the seeds and the environment favorable to the growth of the seeds. These are the qualities of compassion and selflessness instead of *aham mameti*, the selfish reflections related to "I" and "mine."

Bhakti Begins with Faith

> *"The Srimad-Bhagavatam 11.2.42 declares, bhaktih paresanubhavo viraktir anyatra caisa trika eka-kalah, that along with devotional surrender and direct perception of the Supreme*

Lord, aversion to, and detachment from, matter occur simultaneously. This supports the principles discussed earlier that sadhana-bhakti destroys distress and bestows good fortune."
Bhakti Trilogy, 15

Although both of these leaves of *sadhana-bhakti* sprout at the same time, their growth slightly differs. There is a lapse between the removal of distress and the bestowal of good fortune. Devotional service or Bhakti-devi eradicates distress and also brings great fortune but not simultaneously. A problem may arise since we are first freed from some of the difficulties but we have not yet developed the higher taste. Sometimes there is an interim period before we develop the higher taste. It will come with proper perseverance. This transitional period may be challenging for us because these days we have the tendency to constantly look for quick reciprocation on our own time scheme.

Consequently our faith may not be so strong. If we stop our efforts when the immediate reciprocation does not come, we can lose faith and think that it does not work. Faith is very important, especially while undergoing transitions or moving from one level to the next. Faith is, of course, supported by healthy association.

"Bhakti begins with faith. The pilgrim undertaking a journey on

> *the path of devotion must have faith (sraddha), a faith synonymous with the firm conviction to act on the words and the instructions of devotional scriptures. Faith is of two kinds: svabhaviki (natural) and balotpadika (inspired by an external force)."*
>
> Bhakti Trilogy, 16

Natural faith relates to our credits from previous lives, which will ignite with the activities in the immediate environment. The qualities that are an integral part of our inner being come together with external factors to produce a certain quality of faith. The external manifests through good association, since *bhakti* is mainly found in the heart of the unalloyed *bhakta*.

> *"Sincerely following the spiritual master's instructions bestows upon a disciple the good fortune of wanting to associate with an elevated saint experienced and absorbed in the same devotional mood as the disciple himself aspires for—in other words, a like-minded saintly instructor."*
>
> Bhakti Trilogy, 16

This, of course, is the process of devotional service or *bhajana-kriya*, which ultimately leads to *ruci* and *prema*.

Unsteadiness in Devotion

> *"Bhajana-kriya is divided into two parts: anisthita (unsteady) and nisthita (steady). When devotional activities are performed on the nisthita platform, there is no fear of deviation or lethargy."*
> Bhakti Trilogy, 16

This means that on the steady platform, there is no fear, duality or degradation. The problem arises with unsteady devotional service. Lastly, we want to examine the unsteady areas of *bhajana-kriya* and the ways in which they appear. We previously looked at the five causes of distress. Now we will examine the six categories on the unsteady platform.

Sudden Enthusiasm

The first is called *utsahamayi* or sudden enthusiasm. Sometimes when a person first joins or comes in contact with the process, they have this burst of zeal and enthusiasm which often stems from pride. They begin to think that they are extremely special and that overnight they will obtain the full results. They have a type of raw enthusiasm. It is enthusiasm, but raw and immature, comparable to a shadow. This can present a problem because after one has to really pay their dues, they may not have the perseverance or determination required.

Lethargy

The second stage is called *ghana-tarala* or sometimes enthusiastic and sometimes lethargic. These problems exist in the neophyte stages. There is a tendency towards *bhoga-tyaga* in which one feels excitement toward certain aspects of devotional life but still tends to act according to sensations and feelings. One vacillates back and forth. These indicate unsteadiness, which adds to the *misra-bhakti* rather than to the platform of *suddha-bhakti*.

Doubts

The third stage is called *vyudha-vikalpa* or a stage when doubts assail one's resolve. For example, one may think, "The scripture says that household life is a dark well; therefore, maybe I should marry but maybe I should not marry." In this stage, one vacillates back and forth. Another person may think, "Maybe I should join the temple, but if I do join, what will my friend think? Maybe I should not join." "Perhaps I should consider traveling to this part of the world in order to serve and study. However, I would be away from my mother and cousins so maybe I will not travel." One definitely has some desire for acceleration in devotion but, at the same time, many other desires fill the consciousness. This is the stage when doubts assail. A person may have some determination but the doubts are actually stronger than the devotion so the person does not really act on the devotion.

Material Sense Enjoyment

Visaya-sangara is the stage of internal tug-of-war with material sense enjoyment.

> *"Visaya-sangara is the stage when conflicting doubts and arguments are resolved in the devotee's heart and he is convinced about the path of renunciation."*
>
> *Bhakti Trilogy, 18*

In the third stage, doubts and vacillation are there but the doubts are actually stronger. In this next stage, although there is still flickering back and forth, the understanding is stronger but one does not yet have the strength to act on the understanding. We may see different points in our own lives in which we had more doubts than faith. Then we reach the point of having more faith but we lack strong determination, and so our senses still pull us excessively. Although we know the proper actions, we fail to carry them out.

> *"Scripture states that just as an object lost in the west cannot be found in the east, similarly, a person engrossed in materialistic activities will never become attached to Krishna. The devotee feels that his desires for sensual enjoyment are forcing him toward fulfilling them,*

> *and so his attraction for chanting and devotional service becomes weak. Therefore he thinks he should immediately discard those desires and wholeheartedly chant the holy name, although even in the process he may sometimes fall victim to sense gratification. The devotee still remains convinced of the scriptural truth that perfection can be achieved through devotional service."*
>
> Bhakti Trilogy, 18

We may know what is proper but the senses and mind still pull us. Even though we may deviate or feel bewildered, our intelligence knows that we have to get out of the slump and continue moving towards the goal. We keep picking ourselves up. This is a level of conscious unfoldment.

Unrealistic Vows

> *"The next stage of unsteady devotional service is niyamaksama, where the devotee vows to increase his devotional activities. He resolves to chant sixty-four rounds daily; offer one hundred prostrated obeisances to the Deities and the Vaisnavas; serve the senior devotees; avoid talking about mundane topics; shun*

> the company of materialistic minded people, and so on. Daily he makes these vows, but at the last moment he is unable to honor them. The difference between *visaya-sangara* and *niyamaksama* is that in the former the devotee is helpless to give up material sense pleasures, and in the latter he is unable to increase and improve his devotional activities."
> *Bhakti Trilogy, 18-19*

Previously the sinful activities or doubts were stronger but now the basic healthy or good association is lacking. He distinctly explains, "He is unable to increase and improve his devotional activities." So we have the intelligence to understand our improper standard but still cannot improve. Ultimately it relates to our desire, because Krishna will give the necessary strength if the desire is strong enough. Also the desire strengthens through proper association and honoring that healthy association.

Adoration & Distinction

The last category is called *taranga-rangini* or the last stage of *anisthita* devotional service.

> "In describing the nature of *bhakti*, it is said that everyone is attracted towards the reservoir of *bhakti*, the devotee. The devotee himself

> *becomes a treasure-house of good qualities and mercy."*
> *Bhakti Trilogy, 19*

This means that the devotion has passed through many of the obstacles and has become somewhat strong and secure. However, this devotee starts to receive adoration, distinction, or fame, which is a last danger. The danger is that the person will start to accept these boons, and this will cause him to again fall down or remain stagnant at that particular level.

> *"These characteristics attract people who, in turn, crown the devotee with wealth, adoration, distinction and position. Although these accolades come to him as by-products of bhakti, they nevertheless may stunt the spontaneous growth of the creeper of devotion if he uses them for his self-aggrandizement."*
> *Bhakti Trilogy, 19*

This problem kills many of our own devotees in important positions. We all go through points of initial stimulation and excitement but then we have to start working on ourselves. All these doubts will arise but gradually we will be able to conquer them. However, we still have to deal with all of the actions that pull us one way or the other. When we finally overcome the sinful activities and understand proper behavior, we still may not feel the higher taste or have the capacity to change our character. We may even reach the point of changing our position, gross as well as subtle, and receive respect for our new level of achievement. At this point, Bhaktidevi really watches to see how much she can come forth in our lives and what we keep as our priorities. People often get stuck at this level. If we remain too long at any level, we will start to regress.

Questions & Answers

Question: Initially we must refrain from improper activities before we develop the higher taste. How do we overcome this stage? Do we become totally steady in our service?

Answer: Yes, we need to remain steady in our service while maintaining the proper consciousness of humility. However, although we can serve steadily, we may obnoxiously abuse others and serve in a condescending mood. We may shop for the *bhoga* or clean the floor every day, but in the process, we hit people with the mop or even shout at them. It depends on much more than just the action.

Question: How can we develop the courage to carefully scrutinize ourselves now that we have heard so much?

Answer: It is not that we necessarily need much courage but we need to have sufficient distaste for the pain. If we feel enough distaste for the distress and pain, we will feel a desperate need to change. We will not want to keep ourselves wallowing in such pain and keep our lives in such anxiety. Life is not just about anxiety. We really need to love ourselves more. Then we will have had enough and will stop torturing ourselves.

Question: How does our *karmic* conditioning relate to these stagnations? Srila Prabhupada is the embodiment of mercy and the embodiment of so many wonderful things that connect us with *bhakti*; however, all the members of his family did not take to *bhakti*.

Answer: Exactly. Srila Prabhupada's own children did almost the opposite by trying to take away the *bhakti*. We went to court after Srila Prabhupada left the planet because his eldest son tried to take over the assets of the entire institution. He claimed that Srila Prabhupada was a businessman and that the ISKCON society was a business; consequently, he should receive all the assets. His own son threatened to take away everything accomplished in Srila Prabhupada's service.

The example of Srila Prabhupada's deviant son is an example of misuse of free will and the power of free will in our lives. There are many other excellent examples such as Prahlada Maharaja who was a pure devotee but whose father, Hiranyakasipu, was a demon. Advaita Acarya had sons who were

The Second Shower of Nectar

impersonalists. Even we who are part and parcel of Krishna express our free will in all kinds of ways. Yes, we have free will and we can use it in different ways. Even Kala Krishnadasa was with Lord Caitanya, the most magnanimous expression of Krishna, but still he had free will and deviated.

We also see the *karmic* factor but we do not just take the *karma* as everything. As Visvanatha Cakravarti explained, there are many levels of *karma* such as mature, about to mature, the seeds and the environment. All of this fills a person's package and determines what they are carrying and who they are. Someone may bring less to the situation, which means that it will be harder, but not impossible.

For instance, our children will receive academic training that may later lead them to the university. If they receive good training, they will perform well and maybe even better than the average children. However, if their training is not sufficient, they will have problems when they attend these schools. If people start with very little, school may overwhelm them to the point that they just drop out. In some cases, certain devotees have come into devotional service with so few credits from previous lifetimes that the challenges seem almost insurmountable. In other cases, excessive challenges may surround certain devotees but they seem almost naive. It is not that they are naive but they are just so fixed. Sometimes a devotee may be so fixed that, instead of slowing them down, the challenges keep them moving faster and faster. This often results from the credits obtained in previous lifetimes as well as the way they process things in this lifetime.

We should never think, "Well, what can I do? It is just my *karma*." Yes, *karma* definitely influences us but Krishna's mercy is causeless. Although this mercy is available for everyone, we distinctly know that we can bring in credits. For this reason, we must also have sufficient mercy because we do not always know what people have been through in previous lives and what they bring to the current table or environment. Despite what they bring to the table, if the table itself is very powerful, they will still have a great sense of productivity. However, if they bring something to the table and the table itself or the environment is not strong, this will lead to problems.

The Third Shower of Nectar

This third chapter of the *Madhurya-Kadambini* discusses *anartha-nivrtti*, the cessation of unwanted desires. *Anartha* means unwanted desires in the heart and *nivrtti* means to cease. *Bhakti* is always about the heart. If *bhakti* is not properly executed, it means that some contamination is present in the heart and is causing some obstruction. When the *bhakti* is pouring out unconditionally with great vibrancy, we understand that no obstructions are present, and the natural presence of the *bhakti* comes forth. Four different types of obstructions hinder *bhakti* and cover it. In some cases, they practically extinguish it. The first kind is called *duskrtottha or anarthas* coming from sinful activities. The second kind is called *sukrtottha* or *anarthas* coming from pious deeds. The third *anartha* is *aparadhottha* or *anarthas* coming from offenses. Finally we have *bhaktyuttha* or *anarthas* connected with our devotional service.

Understanding Karma

As we look at devotional service, we must constantly remind ourselves that we deal with much more than just the present moment. We are constantly dealing with what we have done, who we were, what environments we were connected with, and how we used or abused those situations in previous lives. The soul is eternal. We are appearing on this stage as if we were in a play with Acts I, II and III. We may be watching Act III or Act 1,000,000 due to the million or more bodies that we have inhabited. The soul, the same identity, has been undergoing a great variety of experiences. We are carrying that associated baggage in different ways along with various patterns or residue. For this reason, interpersonal relationships can be difficult. In dealing with any individual, we are really dealing with many personalities or many aspects of personalities that combine together to make one dominant personality.

Some irrational phobias such as a fear of fire, heights or of small places may be prevalent in the present consciousness because of some connection from a previous life. For example, in a previous lifetime someone may have been pushed off a cliff or jumped off a tall building. Now, in their subtle consciousness, they have some great fear of heights that they cannot quite understand. Someone else may have such a tremendous phobia of snakes that even a picture of a snake causes chills. They might have been bitten by a snake and suffered greatly, and this left a deep impression. It is hard for modern sociologists, psychologists and psychiatrists to deal with these issues because they cannot understand the influence of previous lives, nor can they fully understand the influence of the earlier part of this life.

Sinful Activities

We are looking at *anartha-nivrtti* and closely exploring the four categories that interfere and prevent the heart from experiencing its highest expressions. The first kind involves *anarthas* resulting from sinful activities called *duskrtottha*, which continues to unfold and haunt us. We have not yet fully paid our dues for these activities. As *Vaisnavas*, we may seem harsh when it comes to chastisement. We are currently dealing with several issues in relation to punishment. People who act improperly should apologize and should receive a type of chastisement. It may seem harsh that we honor capital punishment, but if someone takes the life of another, we honor the fact that the murderer's life should also be taken. *Avant-garde* thinkers see this as totally improper, and indeed nowadays it is very risky because of improper legal and executive systems. Trying to combine ideal laws with improper systems will certainly create problems. Many people currently in jail or on death row may be innocent. It is dangerous to have automatic capital punishment for those proven guilty by a flawed system of judgment. Traditionally, capital punishment was recommended to free a person from suffering in that lifetime. Otherwise they would have to pay for their crime in the next life or even later. They will have to suffer if they commit murder—the reaction does not simply go away. They will be forgiven but they have to pay the price. Sometimes we cannot understand why certain things happen to us. Now that we are trying to act properly, we may wonder why we continue to have problems in our lives. Sometimes this is the result of some heavy reactions from the past.

One time an Indian gentleman was quite offensive to Srila Prabhupada in his arguments and his mood. Prabhupada very tactfully said, "I must have done something to him in a previous life." Of course this shows Prabhupada's humility but it also reveals how a *Vaisnava* should think. A *Vaisnava* should humbly tolerate offenses to him or herself but should not tolerate offenses against other *Vaisnavas*. The pure devotees do not accept offenses even when a person acts offensively towards them; however, the offender is held accountable because the Lord in the heart does not take such actions lightly. Actually, devotees feel that they deserve their misfortunes due to their improper behavior in the past. They feel regretful that they have caused another person anxiety. For example, when Brghu Muni kicked Lord Visnu, Visnu did not say, "You will never kick anybody again. I will break that foot and the other foot as well." Instead, He replied, "I am sorry that you hurt your foot on My chest." The mentality of a devotee is very unusual and cannot be understood through orthodox means. For this reason, we must be very careful to properly interact with and avoid offending those who sincerely follow this process.

The Third Shower of Nectar

Keep in mind that the first type of unwanted desires are the *anarthas* coming from sinful activities, either past or present. *Prarabdha* are those reactions that have already matured and *aprarabdha* are those that have not come about yet. This unfolding is dynamic in one sense but also scary because everything is recorded and will give some reciprocation. Even when we try to hide deviations or sinful activities in the closet, they will surely catch up with us. On the other hand, all of our investments, devotion, good actions, words or thoughts will also produce results, either immediately or in the future. When someone receives some seemingly unusual good fortune, it often comes from some buildup of previous pious activities. If someone receives a boon, we can understand the influence of the *karmic* factor.

A few years ago in England, the people wanted the head of a major soccer team to step down because of his insight into Vedic culture. He spoke a few words of wisdom that were powerful but not understood. It was delicate. When he mentioned that people's misfortunes are based on *karma*, the people become furious and campaigned against him. The people argued, "How can you say a blind or crippled person is suffering for their actions in a previous life?" The man finally had to step down. Unfortunately, many people are sentimental and do not understand these sciences. This is really an attack on the whole doctrine of *karma* and reincarnation in a country composed of thousands of people from Indian backgrounds and philosophical religious backgrounds who accept these doctrines as an integral part of their world view.

More knowledgeable people should have come forward to explain *karma* properly without sounding so harsh. It sounds harsh to tell a mother who just lost a child in a car accident, "Well, it is just their *karma*!" People will think, "What is wrong with you crazy devotees? What do you mean? Have you no love or sympathy?" If we express *karma* in such harsh ways, it can be misunderstood, but at the same time, how can such occurrences be anything other than *karma*? If we do not accept *karma*, it means that we do not accept the existence of God or His position as the ultimate controller. We will begin to accept that God has no laws or that Krishna cannot really maintain His own kingdom, as if it overwhelms Him.

We hear that *karma* causes various situations, and although we can process events in this way, we still have to deal with the actual issues at hand. When somebody is born in poverty or with a deformity, it is not necessarily bad, because they will not have as many material facilities to distract them in this lifetime. In general, some representations of bad *karma* include legal problems, chronic diseases, lack of education or lack of beauty. These are some general signs but they do not necessarily indicate that someone is suffering from the reactions of their previous sins. For example, everyone gets sick and everyone dies. In terms of legal problems, excessive litigation usually indicates the influence of *karma*. If we understand these influences maturely, we can approach issues with this knowledge in the background. Imagine someone falling down the steps and hitting their head while you stand at the top step and say, "You have some heavy *karma*. Hopefully you don't have any more coming or you may fall even harder the next time." How would you feel in that situation with someone addressing you in such a harsh way? At the same time, we understand that some uniform scheme of reciprocity underlies all situations.

For this reason, we need to be careful about what we do. Someone might be in anxiety because they cannot have a child. There are people who commit suicide because they cannot have children. However, this same person may have had many abortions in a previous lifetime. Krishna gave them so many souls to care for previously but they kept refusing them and eliminating them. In this lifetime, they desperately want a child but they simply cannot have one. While there may be some *karmic* situation behind the scenes, to address the person in this way is harsh—we should be sensitive and supportive when someone is experiencing the fruits of bad *karma*. Whether or not our help will be effective is, of course, also influenced by their *karma*, but we should always try. These are delicate issues.

Christians and other groups sometimes get disturbed with Eastern perspectives, especially this idea of *karma*. They do not realize that by denying *karma*, they become almost atheists. They do not accept that God ultimately controls everything through the agency of *karma*. For instance, why does one particular bank get robbed instead of the other thousand banks? Why did one particular bank teller get shot instead of the other tellers? This also involves the *karmic* factor, which acts according to the owner of the bank, the people present in the bank and even the robbers.

It is fantastic to consider how Krishna is "on the scene" controlling and how everyone is fully accountable. We may seem to get away with cheating, deviation or abuse, but we will eventually receive corresponding results. If you act harshly or crudely to someone, you will receive the same in return at some point. If you are kind, considerate and thoughtful, you will also receive these kind sentiments in return. Therefore, people should be much more sensitive and eager to act properly regardless of the situations or actions of another person. It is important to act properly in order to avoid the negative *karma* that others may experience.

It greatly hurts our movement when devotees make offenses toward each other. The situation becomes even worse when the offended person makes another offense instead of defeating the negativity with higher *bhakti*. Then the offense continues and everyone suffers. When four or five people get into a fight, one person throws a blow, someone else gets a hammer, or someone gets a brick or stick until everyone is bruised. They are all

The Third Shower of Nectar

brothers and sisters, so when the mother enters, she asks, "What is going on?" The big brother says, "Well, I didn't throw the first punch but I threw the second one." The little cousin says, "I simply came in and started talking to them but then they bumped into me. I let them know not to bump into me again. I took the chair and smashed them in the head." They each think, "I am right!" "No, I am right!" This is craziness.

Maya finds so many ways to distract us from dealing with the real issues at hand. This will always occur, because *maya's* duty is to sabotage the genuine *bhakti*. It is *maya's* duty to make the arrangement for Bhakti-devi to either stay away or to enter. *Maya* says, "Bhakti-devi, stay away from those people—they are not ready for you." *Maya* is actually working for Krishna. The same *maya* will say, "I really tested them and they did not open up even once to let me in. Go ahead Bhakti-devi. There is no place for me there. I will go bother somebody else." Krishna consciousness is so simple if we are genuine. However, we continue to have issues and find reasons to lose faith, get distracted, doubt the *acaryas* and even doubt Krishna. *Maya* will say, "Okay, from your past and present experiences, you are currently in this position. So, for many more lifetimes I will continue to work on you. Then, maybe in one lifetime, you may decide to run away from me, and this will make me happy. I am grabbing you and beating you because I want you to run away, but you keep coming, so I will continue to beat you."

It is wonderful to see how Krishna resides in the heart and watches everything. The Lord knows the consciousness and intent of all of our actions. He knows the nature of our *anarthas* and has given us the ability to move through them. Srila Visvanatha Cakravarti is being used to explain these aspects of the devotional process. Although some people read and read, the information only connects superficially with the mind. It does not really register beyond some philosophical discourse. Sometimes you may see the actions of various devotees and wonder if they are even reading and studying the philosophy. If they are reading, how can they act in such a way? In some cases, although they read, they have stagnations from previous lives and from this present lifetime—they remain bound. As we mentioned earlier, there is a level at which we know right from wrong but still cannot act properly. Unless there is sufficient proper association, we will not be able to act upon our knowledge. For this reason, we must have genuine greed to seek higher association. We must understand what higher association is. We must do everything with a sense of compassion and a sense of caring, otherwise the small flame will not ignite or grow. Planting the seed is just the beginning. You then have to water it, nourish it and protect it. As the plant starts growing, the animals and other creatures begin to notice the creeper and threaten its growth. It has to be guarded very carefully in its early stages otherwise the rats, deer or peacocks will eat the entire plant. Planting is only one aspect of gardening. Next, we must nurture the creeper so that we can later harvest the full-grown plant.

Good Karma can be a Distraction

There are sins or *anarthas* from the past that block *bhakti* in the heart. There are *anarthas* from pious deeds, or *sukrtottha*, that also come from the past. Pious deeds refer to the activities that bring some boon or facility for sense gratification. Due to some piety, you may receive wealth or many opportunities for engaging the senses. These activities can preoccupy us to such an extent that even these "good things" become *anarthas*. Some rich people may have attained their wealth due to previous piety but that same wealth can be their greatest enemy, distracting them and preventing them from taking shelter of simplicity and spiritual life. It causes them to not depend on God, since they have some degree of power themselves. They are the *isvaras* or controllers within their own environments. Other people have such wealth but instead they find ways to support devotional service and use their time to absorb themselves in their devotion, build temples, or make arrangements for service. Sometimes we see these attributes in very pious Indian *Vaisnava* businessmen. They may have great wealth, but they also have great humility. They engage in *puja* for two to three hours every day, an hour before work and two hours at night after work. When you visit their office, they have pictures of Krishna everywhere. They are honest and do not smoke, drink or take intoxication. Such people do exist, but they are rare. You realize that this person is not only great in this life but they have also been great in previous lives. They are using their material opulence to enhance the devotion rather than allowing the wealth to obstruct their spiritual life. So, positive *karma* can accelerate our devotional life, but it can also cause stagnation.

Offenses to the Holy Dhamas

Next we have *aparadhottha* or *anarthas* coming from offenses. We know the different categories of offenses such as *nama-aparadha* or *dhama-aparadha*. Holy *dhamas* magnify our offenses. I have seen cases in which people suffer from a chronic disease for the rest of their life or even fall from devotional service. If we study the situation closely, we see that their offenses in the holy *dhama* led to such situations. For this reason, it is recommended that we should not visit a holy *dhama* for more than three days if we are not in the right consciousness. Conversely, the pilgrimage to the holy *dhama* is an integral tenet of the nature of our existence. We are supposed to have great greed and eagerness to live in holy places. If we cannot physically live in such a place, we must constantly maintain the mindset of connecting with such places. At the same time, these holy places can destroy us if we do not respect them properly. To come so close and act improperly can stagnate the creeper and hurt us tremendously. Krishna holds everyone accountable. He gives us

The Third Shower of Nectar

His *darsana* in the holy places and a chance to visit such *tirthas*. Are we going to honor this, embrace it and take advantage of it, or are we going to continue trying to cheat, lifetime after lifetime? We come so close and still try to use the *dhama* for sense gratification. This happens in all the different holy places such as Vrndavana, Hrsikesa, Hardwar, Jerusalem, Mecca, etc. Some people simply visit these places to do business, sell drugs and engage in prostitution or organized crime. Practically every holy *dhama* on the planet has organized crime. *Maya* has become very powerful. The quality of the person determines what they will pick up in the different environments. Someone may visit Vrndavana and only see the poverty. Someone else may bathe in the Yamuna and only see dirty water. Another person may feel exhilaration even before entering the Yamuna due to the wonderful opportunity to bathe in a sacred river. Even before the physical bathing, they have already bathed since their consciousness is absorbed in the environment. The external circumstances are the same, but they can be perceived and codified differently. We cannot blame Krishna. In the wrestling match, people saw the same Krishna differently according to their consciousness, which depended on their *anarthas*, fears and sins or on their freedom from such impediments. Krishna and Balarama make Themselves available to us, but our experience depends on how much we make ourselves available to connect with the Lord.

Knowledge can be Dangerous

Visvanatha Cakravarti makes everything clear. There are distinct factors that cause some of these diseases. For example, all our actions are magnified in the holy *dhama*. If we act properly, we will receive many credits and benefits, but if we act improperly, we will suffer extensively. It is even worse for people to read and discuss such aspects of the process and then continue with the offenses despite their knowledge. For example, if we attend the VIHE programs or different workshops and receive knowledge but still act improperly, the chastisement will be heavy. It is dangerous to know and not to act. Now, more and more of our devotees all over the world know so much. We have so many books, tapes, literatures and pastimes of Srila Prabhupada. So many devotees are writing very nice books and giving wonderful seminars. If people are exposed to more and more but fail to act upon it, the suffering will be greater. For this reason, many devotees are depressed and even suicidal. Krishna consciousness is wonderful and powerful but also extremely dangerous if we do not embrace it and use it properly. We understand that, if a *brahmana* makes an offense, it is worse than an offense made by a first initiated devotee. Furthermore, it is worse for an initiated devotee to make an offense than the new *bhakta*. The more we are supposedly connected with the culture of devotion and are supposedly carriers of this culture, the greater the consequence will be of committing an offense. Therefore, the scriptures state that if a *sannyasi* falls down, it is better to commit suicide. If one comes to the level of representing the system and receiving honor and respect based on one's position as a carrier but then deviates, it would practically be better to take one's own life to free oneself from some of the *karma* that will follow.

The Misery of Falldown

Notice that most of the *sannyasis* in our movement who fall down leave. In other words, the *karmic* reaction is so heavy that most of them cannot get enough footing to participate in the process in this lifetime in a healthy way again. Those who try to continue in the process are very special. Somehow they humbly continue although every day is difficult for them. We do not play games with Krishna. We do not accept the role as a caretaker for people and then abuse that position. By instructing people in one way and acting in the opposite way, your life will simply be a big lie. *Maya* will say, "You are in my camp now; therefore, I will deal with you appropriately. Since you are not properly protected and your actions have brought you to my camp, I now have the chance to deal with you." This is very dangerous. It is even worse to fall into *maya* after hearing this knowledge. Then, every time the person engages in some sinful activity, the intelligence will just beat them. Whatever temporary pleasures they experience will simply be followed by hellish suffering. It is harsh to have so many people in knowledge who cannot follow or are unwilling to follow. However, we should feel sad that one of our brothers, sisters, nieces, nephews, aunts or uncles is in such a devastating situation. Imagine an extreme case in which your relative is living in the streets and eating out of garbage cans. You think, "This is my aunt or brother who is roaming around out there like a mad person." You should feel very bad. We should also feel very bad that some people have come to this process and heard the knowledge but, due to various weaknesses, they are not following the science or having proper association. Due to some obstacles from the past that might weigh them down, they are not working hard enough to move beyond them. When they return to their old patterns, they actually suffer more than they otherwise would have, due to their knowledge.

If you took initiation and made vows but are now taking drugs, engaging in illicit sex, and going against the instructions of *guru* and the *Vaisnavas*, you are suffering and you know you are suffering. You are not ready to change but, at the same time, you really want to be different. Although you may try, you do not have sufficient determination. That is hell. I have never experienced it and I hope that I never will, but by just thinking about such a situation, we can understand the nature of such a hell. It means knowing that you are a cheater, your life is a lie, and you are actually an embarrassment to one of the greatest expansions of Krishna's mercy. We all have to do our part to keep people away from those situations. We keep them away by not getting caught up in other people's nonsense or not overreacting and under reacting to different occurrences. We also should not go into denial or become frantic as if Krishna is not there. We do have sadness that people are not following properly and are going to suffer for their sins. Most important, we must live our lives in such ways that our lives become our message. The greatest way to serve the *Vaisnava* community is to act like a *Vaisnava*. You can lecture, write papers or send e-mails everywhere, but the greatest service is to act as a *Vaisnava* in all circumstances. When people come around you, they have to act as *Vaisnavas* because your existence indicates that you will only engage in *Vaisnava* activities and conversations. Therefore, reminding others as well as ourselves of our particular commission becomes the greatest offering. *Maya* distracts us in many ways, so Srila Visvanatha Cakravarti discusses these *anarthas* and how they manifest in order to help us remain focused.

Anarthas from Devotional Service

The last category, called *bhaktyuttha* means *anarthas* coming from devotional service. First we have *anarthas* coming from sinful activities, past and present. Secondly we have *anarthas* coming from pious activities. Then there are *anarthas* coming from all different types of offenses. Last we have *anarthas* coming from devotional service such as *lobha*, *puja* and *pratistha*. When Lord Caitanya was cleaning the Gundica temple and uprooting the subtle dirt, He was addressing these types of *anarthas*. These *anarthas* are more subtle than the others. We may have transcended the other impediments, but we still have to closely examine our desires for distinction and adoration or our interest in pride. After you have nicely performed a service, you now have this pride or condescending mood. "I have been there. I know this." *Maya* says, "Okay, you have been there. You know this. I have a special one for people like you." *Maya* has a special way to deal with you. "You feel you have mastered me. You do not have sufficient fear of me." This can cause problems because there can be no imperfections in the spiritual world. Although we may engage in so many services, we still have to give up the idea that we are responsible and are to be glorified. *Maya* arranges ways to expose the situation or the person so that they can deal with these last types of *anarthas*. We want to reflect on these four types of *anarthas*. If we have a clear understanding of what to avoid and how to remove the unhealthy impediments, we are left with divine and positive qualities.

Srila Visvanatha Cakravarti goes on to explain certain aspects of *seva-aparadha*. In summary, he explains that the chanting of the holy name is so powerful that, although we will continue to commit offenses until we are pure, the offenses are not as serious if we have good intentions. We may not dress the Deities in such a wonderful way but hopefully the heart and mind are in the right place. For example, we may forget to put the *camara* in the Deity's hand but these are only slight obstacles and will not cause any serious stagnation. If one is serving and chanting the holy name, Krishna receives and accepts the service. If a child tries to paint a picture and works with genuine love, although he or she cannot paint well, the child acted with love for us to receive and accept. When we receive the picture, we feel happy even though it is still wet, and the paint gets all over our hands and clothing.

> *"The holy name of Krishna is all-powerful and can absolve any offense, however serious. The offender may incorrectly think, 'If this is true about chanting, then why should I have to fall at the Vaisnava's feet in such a humble manner and demean myself?' After all, the scriptures ensure that for one who commits nama aparadha chanting on its own will clear away all offenses, hence I shall certainly be again pardoned.' Such thinking is incorrect. Instead the offender becomes enmeshed in another heinous nama aparadha, that of committing sin on the strength of chanting the holy name."*
> Bhakti Trilogy, 23

This mentality really shows the person's lack of genuine compunction or regret. They are not ready to approach the person and beg for forgiveness. Although they may feel slightly upset, if they really felt compunction or sadness, they would have the genuine humility to sincerely ask for forgiveness. Instead, they just want freedom from the reaction and think that a few extra rounds of chanting will suffice. One cannot so easily eradicate the offense in this way.

> *"Instead, the offender becomes enmeshed in another heinous nama aparadha, that of committing sin on the strength of chanting the holy name."*
>
> Bhakti Trilogy, 23

If they recognize their *aparadha* but remain unwilling to beg for forgiveness, it indicates the presence of a large false ego. They lack a real sense of regret. Furthermore, they think, "I will just chant the holy name to clear myself of the offense." Using the holy name to clear away sinful activities is simply another type of *aparadha*. If we think chanting will erase the sin, we become more prone to again engage in sinful activities. When you offend someone, you have the responsibility to humbly submit yourself to that person. This submission can act as a deterrent against committing further offenses due to embarrassment and anxiety. This is the seventh offense; that is, committing sinful activities on the strength of chanting the holy name of the Lord.

Offending Each Other

If we are not careful, one offense often leads to another. This happens in devotees' lives when they take certain things for granted or make offenses without having the proper humility. Later, it turns into *guru-aparadha* and they even start doubting Srila Prabhupada. Next it turns into *Krishna-aparadha* to the point that they doubt Krishna and the whole process. This process is a science. If we follow the science properly, we will obtain certain results.

> "The offender may once again try to rationalize his misbehavior by saying, 'According to the scriptures (SB 11.11.29) only those who are compassionate, peaceful, and tolerant are called sadhus, or saintly persons. Therefore, the offense of blaspheming a devotee is appropriate only when someone who possesses these characteristics is criticized, not for one who has not developed these qualities.'"
>
> Bhakti Trilogy, 23

We may understand that blasphemy of a devotee is an offense but may not really see the *mataji*, the *brahmacari*, the temple commander, or the devotees in our direct association as *sadhus*. Therefore, they will not feel the need to apologize to such people and will rationalize the offense in this way.

If you offend a devotee and apologize but he or she gives you the cold shoulder, you may feel discouraged. You may think, "I have done my part. This person is not a *sadhu* anyway. What can I do?" However, the scripture states that, if someone does not immediately accept the apology, we should still approach and try to humble ourselves. We should not see the situation as hopeless. We should feel, "It is so unfortunate that I have made such an offense which now follows me. I cannot be forgiven. Let me try to approach in a more sincere way. Let me use this as Krishna's arrangement to help me better understand the seriousness of my improper actions. Let me use this as a deterrent against future offenses." We do not deny the offense, chant to clear ourselves, or feel that we have done our part—we must continue in the process.

Srila Visvanatha Cakravarti Thakura then talks about the *jiva*.

> "The jiva's position is that of eternal loving servitorship to the Supreme Personality of Godhead. Jiva is of two categories, the first category being those under the spell of illusion and nescience. Demigods, humans, animals and lesser beings are in the first category of jivas. The second kind, those who are free from nescience and illusion, are subdivided into two sections.

> 1) Those who are absorbed in the opulence of the Supreme Lord and worship Him reverentially. 2) Those who are neither attracted to the Lord's opulence nor to this mood of reverential worship.
>
> "The jivas who are unattracted to the opulence of the Lord are also further divided. 1)Those who cultivate jnana (speculative knowledge) and desire to merge with the Supreme Lord. 2) Those who mechanically perform devotional activities (sadhana-bhakti) but who have no desire to merge with the Lord."
>
> Bhakti Trilogy, 26

Even though we have come to the devotional process and are experiencing some initial aspect of Bhakti-devi, if we are mechanical or too caught up in mental speculation, there will be stagnation and the *anarthas* will not be removed.

Breaking Free

We can mitigate the four *anarthas* mentioned in the beginning of this chapter in five ways. We first talked about the nature of the different *anarthas* and will finish this section by discussing how to stop these *anarthas* and the natural process that helps them to gradually fall to the side. *Ekadesavarttini* is when the *anartha* is partially destroyed. *Bahu-*

desavarttini means that the *anartha* is substantially destroyed, freed or erased. *Prayiki* is when the *anartha* is almost completely destroyed. *Purna* is when the *anartha* is totally destroyed. *Atyantiki* means that the *anartha* is absolutely, thoroughly destroyed at which point one has love of God.

> *"The many anarthas stemming from aparadhas are partially destroyed in the final stages of bhajana-kriya (rendering devotional service under the guidance of a spiritual master)...When bhajana-kriya gains maturity it turns to nistha, or steadiness, in devotional activities. In this stage of development the mitigation of anarthas is substantial (bahu-desavarttini); thereafter, on the platform of rati (attraction) the unwanted desires in the heart are almost completely absolved (prayiki). With the first awakening of prema, or divine love, these anarthas are completely removed (purna)."*
>
> *Bhakti Trilogy, 29*

When this *prema* is established, the *anarthas* are completely destroyed. We are pleasure seekers, always engaged in different kinds of activities, exchanges, relationships and reflections. As we become more absorbed in the process of *sadhana-*

The Third Shower of Nectar

bhakti, these improper stagnations move to the side. Our faith develops and we proceed with good *sadhu-sanga*. We now participate in *bhajana-kriya* and engage in the regulative principles under good guidance. Gradually we develop this steadiness and taste. It continues on and on. As these stages develop, the ecstasy and realizations burn up the weeds and seeds and even affect the environment so that weeds cannot ever be planted again. Gradually that ecstasy, which is a shadow and reflection of the real love, becomes an integral part of our being. When a person becomes more Krishna conscious, they have no desire to associate with or tolerate any craziness. It is out of their realm. For instance, if someone offered you a hamburger, you would say, "No way! Are you crazy?" Due to the ecstasy, we become so enthused and full that other allurements cannot interest us. The ecstasy just burns up any improper contaminations. As they get more and more burnt away, the atmosphere clears and the creeper, the *bhakti-lata-bija*, is fully situated in *prema*.

This simply means that the lust has now been converted into love. The beauty is that the love was always there, but simply needed to be converted. The intensity is there. We are always going to be mad, but mad after what? Mad after *maya* or mad after Krishna? Now the channel has been adjusted. Before, we were eating, sleeping, mating and defending for the "big me" but now we engage in all of these activities for Krishna. In the past, we sang songs and read mundane literature but now, it is all for Krishna. When we empty ourselves by allowing this creeper to develop and to push out the contaminations, the *anarthas* no longer interfere. First it is partial and then it is almost complete. Next it is complete and then it becomes total absorption to the point that the *anarthas* cannot sneak in again.

Trusting the Lord

Sometimes people think that one who has advanced to the highest level or received the *darsana* of the Lord can still have sins following them from a previous life or still remain under the effects of *karma*. At times certain advanced personalities may undergo unusual circumstances but this occurs due to the Lord's special mercy in which He removes certain attachments or obstacles in order to benedict the person. Krishna may even put a person in poverty in order to bestow greater boons on them. *Srimad-Bhagavatam* 10.88.8 states:

> *yasyaham anugrhnami*
> *harisye tad-dhanam sanaih*
> *tato 'dhanam tyajanty asya*
> *svajana duhkha-duhkhitam*

> "If I especially favor someone, I gradually deprive him of his wealth. Then the relatives and friends of such a poverty-stricken man abandon him. In this way he suffers one distress after another."

In another place, the Lord says, *nirdhanatva-maharogo mad anugraha-laksanam*, "The awesome affliction known as poverty is in fact a sign of mercy."

Sometimes *Akincana-Krishna* takes everything away. It is not due to previous *karma*, past sins or seeds but it is due to a special benediction. Srila Visvanatha offers us such a wonderful message. The message is the same as those of the previous *acaryas* but the different great servants of the Lord have their own ways of expressing their love for humanity and executing their services to their spiritual masters. Although *maya* is the same in this millennium, the next millennium, and in the previous millennia, it surfaces in many different ways. It is no secret how *maya* manifests or how to counteract *maya*. One of the really beautiful aspects of Krishna consciousness is that we have this constant living history. We do not just read *Bhagavad-gita* and think, "Arjuna and Krishna are pretty far out. It is a nice epic about what they used to do then and how they performed their activities in the past." No. Even though these pastimes occurred many hundreds of years ago or even in other *yugas*, they remain ever fresh and ever available for us today.

Questions & Answers

Question: In our interactions with different devotees, sometimes the relationships improve. However, it could result from our own improvement or also from the other person's improvement. How can we prevent ourselves from thinking that we are the ones who improved?

Answer: This is one of the issues we have been discussing in relation to pride. First we talked about mercy and effort. One should not think, "Just see how nicely I grabbed the rope." In the same way, one should also not think, "I am so wonderful that I changed this person." We must be careful to always approach situations with a sense of humility, especially when we succeed or achieve. In such cases, it is even more important to access humility. Of course, it is easier to maintain humility when we get smacked in the face or when events foil our plans, since we cannot maintain the illusion of control. It can bring a certain natural humility. When we do seem to have control, it indicates the presence of a dangerous illusion. It is very hard for rich people to take to spiritual life because, if someone is not suffering as much and has power and money, they may think, "Why do I have to take shelter of God? I can just pay money to fulfill my desires. I can simply use my contacts." In this category, opulence and wealth become distractions and the pious deeds or benefits from the past become the greatest obstacles. If we have some problems or arguments in a relationship, which we later resolve, we should not think, "I acted so wonderfully and tolerated the person so expertly that they have now changed. I am so wonderful that I finally straightened them out. I am really a *sadhu* and a good philosopher also." Actually we should think, "How fallen I am that the whole issue came up in the first place. It is so wonderful that we can now relate better. It is certainly based on Srila Prabhupada's mercy that we have been brought together in this way. Now I must be careful to not let this conflict happen again to someone else." If we have this kind of humility, life moves fast for us. We will be much happier and fixed in our devotion. We will not be caught by the last category of *anarthas* such as *puja*, *lobha* and *pratistha*, which are the final snares. When we are situated properly and involved in a productive situation that brings results, claiming proprietorship will bring us back down again.

Question: Once, while a devotee and I were talking, I asked if I had offended another devotee. He said that he was a *Vaisnava* and did not take offense. However, it seems that even if a devotee does not feel offended, there would still be some reaction because Krishna sees the offense.

Answer: Yes, an offense was made. Since the person may be a *Vaisnava*, he or she did not personally accept it but an offense has been registered. The person who they offended may not accept it or even may humbly see it as their own fault. The Lord in the heart has marked it as an offense and the person must be accountable and pay the necessary dues.

Question: I did not really understand your discussion about the deleting of the different *anarthas*. The last two were 'completely' and 'absolutely thoroughly.' I do not understand the difference.

Answer: It is comparable to a point of no return. At such a point, one has 'absolutely thoroughly' been accepted by Krishna and is in blissful exchange with the Lord in their original *svarupa*. There is no question of any deviation or lack of absorption in Krishna. We are all for Krishna and Krishna is all for us.

Question: Are the results or reactions of these offenses or *anarthas* also the Lord's mercy?

Answer: When you put your hand in fire and burn yourself, it indicates that the fire is hot and dangerous. In this sense, the reactions are mercy because they help us to understand the effects of that situation. Hopefully, you will not put your hand in the fire again.

Question: When we make a mistake or acknowledge an improper behavior, how can we bring ourselves to actually desire to correct ourselves and come to grips with the error?

Answer: Some people can only learn from the failure, from the whipping, and from the hard knocks. Some lessons we definitely learn from hearing and other lessons we learn from seeing. Especially when we are dull or stagnant, we may learn more from experience. Although this is the slow, difficult and dangerous method, some people need to learn in this way. Krishna knows this and allows people to learn in these different ways. As we said earlier, we still should not say, "Well, it is just *karma*. That person will only learn by really getting smashed." We should still do our part but, at the same time, if someone is having the experience, getting chastised, and not changing, we can understand the influence of *karma*. We should recognize the *karmic* factor because Krishna will always provide the help if we really want it. If we make offenses but really want to stop, Krishna will provide a way to help us recognize our offenses in order to stop them. If we do not have this genuine *adhikara* and really want to stop, then we will not change until certain situations actually force us to change. Even then some people do not change. The worst case is when they receive chastisement but, instead of changing, they blame everyone else. When one acts in such a way, it is only a matter of time before Radharani moves them out of the way.

Question: Visvanatha Cakravarti demonstrated how to deal with pride through his own life. He explained that at one point he served in a school and received aggrandizement from the people in the village. He felt that he was becoming proud because of this glorification and felt the need to leave the place. In terms of my own prideful nature, in order to leave that place of pride, it seems that the activities have to manifest first for me to understand it as a prideful activity. How do we work on this pride without having to undergo an experience that results in chastisement or pain?

Answer: We just have to appreciate others more. If we really appreciate other *Vaisnavas* more, how can we have pride? Pride deals with some condescending mood. If we have too much pride, we are condescending. We think of ourselves as better than others, which means that we see others as lower than ourselves. If we have better genuine feelings for others, we will have less pride. If not, then the opposite happens and Krishna smashes us. When we chant and try, but still hold on to some improper contaminations, Krishna helps us. When we chant, we are saying, "Dear Krishna, please use me, engage me in Your service, and help me." If He tries to help us in obvious ways but we do not receive the help, at such a point He smashes us as a way to help us. The main factor lies in having greater appreciation for others.

We do not have to specifically know all of the *anarthas, aparadhas* and weaknesses. It is good for us to try to understand them, but if we simply have greater appreciation for *sadhus*, these obstacles will not enter our consciousness. Any issues will be easily eradicated because of our genuine sense of appreciation. When we lack this appreciation, we will become mechanical. We can even offer apologies but we will not really mean it. We will continue to act in the same way or even worse at a later time because we will not really be respecting and honoring the other person's existence. This means we are thinking more in a *karma-kanda* way. We may simply try to clear ourselves from an offense in order to become a greater devotee. Even though an apology may be there, it is not real appreciation. If we really honor another person's existence, we are careful to avoid improper behavior and are genuinely regretful when we do act improperly. If we come in this mood, Krishna gives us the intelligence to avoid future mistakes.

The Fourth Shower of Nectar

In the *Fourth Shower of Nectar,* Srila Visvanatha Cakravarti discusses the different types of obstacles in devotional service that we must remove in order to really experience the higher connections with the spiritual world and with Krishna. We will focus on *bhajana-kriya* performed on the steady, or *nisthita,* platform and the five obstacles that hinder the development of steadiness.

> "Once the anarthas are removed, then these five obstacles are almost abolished and devotion becomes firm and undeviating. Therefore it can be said that the absence of these five impediments in the heart are symptoms of nisthita-bhakti."
> Bhakti Trilogy, 36

Sleep During Hearing and Chanting

The first obstacle is known as *laya.* "*Laya* is the weakness of being more soporific during hearing about the Lord than while chanting His names, and more soporific while remembering Lord Hari than during hearing about Him" (*Bhakti Trilogy*, 36). This obstacle manifests as the tendency to sleep during *kirtana, sravana* and *smarana* or, in other words, the tendency to sleep during chanting, hearing and remembering the Lord. This first obstacle is a type of dullness that interferes with the devotion. When we do not feel enthused in devotional service, certain desires become more prominent and we begin to give more attention to all the bodily concerns. We will want to eat and sleep more or will feel more sexually agitated. It seems as if all the senses become amplified in their desires for sensual stimulation and pleasure. For example, when you are bored, you may notice the tendency to eat to fill the emptiness. Overeating indicates emptiness and the desire for fulfillment, stimulation, pleasure and love. A part of your being wants nourishment, and if it does not come from the psychological or spiritual, you will focus on the physical. Some people engage in so many extracurricular activities in order to fill up a serious emptiness in their lives. They constantly involve themselves in physical activities to try and forget the extent of their suffering. Other people are workaholics. They find many ways to keep busy and even when they come home, they continue working to avoid dealing with the realities in their lives. They try to cloud their whole life and consciousness with external activities.

Speaking or Thinking Mundane Nonsense

The second obstacle is known as *viksepa*.

"*Viksepa* is talking or thinking about mundane nonsense during devotional activities such as hearing or chanting" (*Bhakti Trilogy*, 36). We see this not only in the temples but also in the churches, mosques or synagogues. Although people bring their bodies to the temple and participate in the worship ceremony, they do not bring their minds. They gossip and engage in small talk despite the discourse. They come mechanically for the ritual and the service, but their consciousness is not in tune. Even though they could benefit from the internal spiritual nourishment, there is obfuscation because they are not really accepting it fully.

Feeling Incapable or Disinterested

The third obstacle is known as *apratipatti*. "*Apratipatti* is when both *laya* and *viksepa* are absent, but at times one still feels incapable of, or disinterested in, hearing, chanting and so on" (*Bhakti Trilogy*, 36). This relates to a failure type of mentality. Sometimes people have a mentality of defeat or lack of self-worth, and even when they have chances to genuinely accelerate, they do not accept it because they continue to think of themselves as failures. This may manifest as co-dependency or lack of self-esteem but for spiritualists it often deals with a lack of faith in God. We can feel some weakness or humility within ourselves—that is appropriate—but we should not feel that anything is beyond Krishna's help or assistance. A devotee understands the need for effort but also the importance of mercy. We do not rely solely on effort, nor do we just wait for the mercy. They must go hand in hand. Krishna says that as we surrender He rewards accordingly.

Acting with the Wrong Consciousness

The fourth obstacle is known as *kasaya*. "Kasaya is defined as the tendency to display such faults as anger, greed, and arrogance during devotional activities" (*Bhakti Trilogy*, 36). We understand this as a certain type of *seva-aparadha*. We may physically engage in certain services but act with the wrong consciousness. For example, when we enter the temple or Deity kitchen, we recognize it as a sacred place. We may have different anxieties and frustrations, but when we come into the sacred facility, we should honor it in the proper way. We should see it as an opportunity for cleansing, refocusing and honoring the higher. Entering the kitchen to cook involves more than combining certain ingredients. It is a chance to prepare an offering for the Lord and the devotees, which means that consciousness, devotion and love are the important factors. Also, the *pujari* who dresses the Deities should think, "I must not bring a contaminated consciousness into this service because not only will I minimize the importance of this opportunity, but my consciousness will reverberate throughout the environment."

Deity service and the quality of the cooking are two major services that amplify and affect the environment. Even the materialists have a general idea of the ability to affect a person's heart through food, but they do not realize the seriousness and profundity of this fact. Sometimes the conflicts in a temple or project may stem from cooks who are not preparing the food with devotion, love and care. Consequently, their energy and consciousness enter the foodstuff and has a way of amplifying and affecting the general atmosphere. The same effect can occur with the Deity service. If one does not serve carefully and dresses or touches the Lord without devotion, care and compassion, this consciousness also has its way of dispersing itself into the environment.

On the other hand, it is wonderful when the cooks prepare the foodstuff with care, devotion and love. Not only will it taste delicious, but the devotion will also add a metaphysical and spiritual aspect to the food, increasing its quality of mercy. Everyone knows this indirectly. Sometimes if you eat a meal prepared extemporaneously, with a lack of real care, you will get sick afterwards. People eat fast food on a regular basis without realizing the dangerous effect on their consciousness. The food is not offered to the Lord, it is bad for their physical and spiritual heath, and it is prepared in such a massive way that it just bombards people with greed, avariciousness, lust and fears. Then they wonder why it is so hard to maintain a sense of stability within themselves and why so much difficulty arises in their relationships. This sort of energy constantly radiates and vibrates. For these reasons, we often find that highly evolved, spiritual people are extremely selective about the type of food they eat and the environments in which they eat. Even the atmosphere affects the consciousness. The *Srimad-Bhagavatam* provides information about all aspects of the *karmic* effect. The person who prepares the food, the person who eats the food and even the atmosphere are all affected. In the case of flesh, the person who kills the animal, the person who transports the meat, the person who cooks it and the person who eats it are all *karmically* responsible. For example, during a bank robbery, many people play specific roles such as the robber, the person who drove the car, the person who drew the gun and the person who shot the teller. One individual may say, "I didn't shoot anyone so I'm innocent." However, that same "innocent" person drove the car that took the murderer to the bank, which means that he or she directly assisted in the killing. Of course there are mitigating factors that will determine the degree of guilt and involvement but each person is a part of the crime.

Attachment to Sense Pleasure

The fifth obstacle to firm and undeviating devotion is known as *rasasvada*. "*Rasasvada* means that the mind is so attached to sense pleasure, often meditating on it, that he is unable to hear and chant with concentration" (*Bhakti Trilogy*, 36). In this case, the mind is so absorbed in reflections on sensual gratification that it appears like a screen to haunt the person. They are so engrossed in these mindsets that it completely prevents them from benefiting from the devotional environment.

Thoughts, Words, Actions

Next Srila Visvanatha Cakravarti speaks about faith. *Nistha* (fixed faith) has two varieties: *saksat bhakti-visayini*, or nourishing spontaneous *bhakti*, and *vastu-visayini*, or the fostering of complementary *bhakti* qualities. One is spontaneous and natural and the other is complementary. He goes on to explain that this spontaneous *bhakti* has three categories: physical *(kayiki)*, oral *(vaciki)* and mental *(manasiki)*. This is similar to the different types of offenses; however, offenses start from the mental as we process the environment and deal with our perceptions. Improper thoughts turn into improper speech. You may hold some unhealthy mentality and continue thinking and reflecting, "Why did she do that? Why did he do that? What right does he have to say that to me? This is the third time she has done this. I cannot take it anymore." Next you begin speaking harshly because the internal conversation will eventually turn into external actions. Or maybe you internalize such feelings as envy, jealousy, anger or hurt, which later come out in speech. If you keep talking and gossiping about people, next you will start to act in such ways. Our thoughts should be of such a nature that we are ready to honor them in speech and in action.

If we constantly reflect on devotional and uplifting thoughts and think positively about other people, we can assist, serve and help in wonderful ways. Next we will start talking positively during our interactions, which will lead to the formulation of ideas and then the actualization of those plans and ideas. Obviously many of our actions stem from a certain type of consciousness that then produces a specific type of vocal activity. Actually, everything that transpires is connected with a certain quality of consciousness. A negative type of consciousness produces tribalism, racism, chauvinism and religious fanaticism. Conversely, a positive, loving consciousness produces auspiciousness in our relationships with others. Everything goes back to the consciousness factor. As we work on transforming our consciousness, we change society by changing ourselves first. Then, if we think differently, we will begin to speak differently which will lead to different actions.

Change Physical Actions

Srila Visvanatha Cakravarti talks about faith in this way: "Some say that there is a definite order of development in these three divisions of *saksat-bhakti*. The devotee first cultivates spontaneous *bhakti* with *kayiki*, followed by *vaciki* and *manasiki* respectively. The opposing group, however, contends that there is no such successive order" (*Bhakti Trilogy*, 37). Due to our conditioning, we are not full lovers of God; therefore, our speech and thoughts are not very pure. What should we do? We try to work on a consciousness shift; however, our consciousness has been stuck for some time. Therefore we change our physical activity, which will change our speech and thoughts. For example, Upendra dasa, a servant of Srila Prabhupada, felt that offering obeisances to

The Fourth Shower of Nectar

some of his godbrothers was somewhat artificial if he did not have genuinely good feelings about them. He asked Srila Prabhupada why he should prostrate himself before certain devotees without feeling kindness or love towards them. Prabhupada said that we should act properly even if the thoughts may not fully correspond because as we perform the action it will gradually affect our thinking. There may be tension between two devotees and then one devotee just offers obeisances and apologizes. Even though the other person tries to be hard and not give in, it just melts the person's heart. It creates a whole shift in energy because someone tries to accelerate the higher, which makes a shift in consciousness. We may feel disturbed about a situation but we should first try to understand the feelings of another before we attempt to be understood. How does the other person feel? How does the other person understand the situation? Then it makes a whole shift in the relationship because we have now made an alteration in our consciousness. The other person will experience it and feel it both consciously and subconsciously.

Since we have found so many amazing ways to avoid surrendering to the Lord and have been thinking and speaking accordingly lifetime after lifetime, it will not be easy to immediately change our consciousness. Therefore, we can approach this predicament from another direction by at least changing our physical actions. As a result, we will begin to speak more about divinity and speak positively about *sadhus*, which will cause us to lose the desire to speak of other topics. After the actions are proper and the speech becomes proper, then the mind will begin to change as well. As the mind begins to change, gradually we start living more in the internal than the external. Eventually we begin to experience the internal to such an extent that we fully identify ourselves as a spiritual being while the physical remains in the background.

Humility, Friendliness, Compassion

> *"Furthermore, qualities such as humility, which specifically means renouncing respect given to the self by others but still offering respect to others, friendliness and compassion are conducive to the culture of devotional service."*
>
> Bhakti Trilogy, 37-38

Humility means that we do not need respect or honor but, at the same time, we feel eager to respect others. There is great strength in humility. It is not a lack of self-esteem, where we remain in a weak position. Rather we humble ourselves by honoring others, appreciating life and appreciating what Krishna has done for us. It is a matter of gratitude and appreciation. Offering respect to others, friendliness and compassion are conducive to the culture of devotional service.

The Fourth Shower of Nectar

> *"Sometimes it appears that certain devotees who are self-controlled and equipoised possess these qualities, although they lack bhakti-nistha, or unwavering faith in devotional service."*
>
> Bhakti Trilogy, 38

This statement is slightly complex. What does this mean? Sometimes a person seems to be righteous and ethical but has no connection with religion or spirituality. This person may have a good heart and genuine piety but, due to some hypocrisy, they have not embraced the theistic position or the idea of a Godhead. At other times, it may result from some intense level of religiosity and spirituality from a previous life so, even though they may not fully honor it in this lifetime, it still remains a strong part of their behavior. Another person may be very religious and even follow all the external rituals but he or she is very passionate, selfish, obnoxious and even argumentative. Someone else may be an expert in speaking scripture but very bad in terms of relationships. In many cases, this simply shows the different ways the modes of material nature unfold. We can perform one activity in the mode of goodness, one in the mode of passion and another activity in the mode of ignorance.

Devotees often display many varieties of characteristics and some people may even feel surprised after discovering so many types of devotees. They may think, "Well, if you come into this type of process, then surely you must be a saint". However, in any institution, you have people who closely and genuinely follow the instructions and you have those who are lackadaisical and whimsical. Some people are complete hypocrites and cheaters. These people have a way of sabotaging the process in any religious organization because they confuse what is genuine. Every institution has these types of people. Someone may think, "How could an institution with such a high philosophy have these problems?" However, people have their free will, and as they enter various situations they carry aspects of their past, including the choice to avoid taking their medicine. Or the medicine may be available but they only take it occasionally or maybe forget the medicine altogether. These actions lead to different consequences.

The Bhakti Yardstick

> "His consciousness, thus purified of evil traits like lust, then becomes fixed in the mode of goodness and the devotee experiences divine happiness. The essential yardstick for measuring perfectly the depth of nisthita-bhakti, or the lack of it (anisthita-bhakti), is whether hearing and chanting has intensified or has stagnated."
>
> *Bhakti Trilogy, 38*

The Fourth Shower of Nectar

We use this as a barometer to determine the degree of *anarthas* or *aparadhas* in our devotional life. If too many weeds or distractions fill our heart, hearing and chanting will become more difficult and we will feel stagnant and lose our taste. This indicates that the devotional creeper is under attack or covered over. The increase of hearing and chanting thus indicates a rise in *nisthita-bhakti* and a decrease implies the presence of *anisthita* or the presence of different types of *anarthas*. For these reasons, regulation is important. We will not be as affected by changes in the mind and environment if we are regulated. The mind and body will continue to move according to a certain scheme despite the incoherence. However, if we are not regulated, the constant shifts and duality in the environment will force us to move with the current. For example, if you are trying to move upward but the current pushes against you, it will gradually pull you down. If you are moving upward against the current and somehow stabilizing yourself, the current will not affect you in the same way because of your stability. The regulations give us some stability despite the assaults from the mind, environment, demigods and other people. It is dangerous when we start losing our regulation. *Maya* will have a greater chance to grab you and push you. Conversely, the danger of regulation is that we will simply act mechanically—chanting, praying or meditating at specific times without connecting with the essence. We must be careful to avoid this as well. When people act mechanically without involving their hearts and minds, they will not receive the proper nourishment because God cannot be bribed, ingratiated or flattered. He is looking at our consciousness and our heart.

Questions & Answers

Question: Is it not true that the entire process of *sadhana-bhakti* is engaging in devotional service mechanically? For in *sadhana-bhakti* one is doing most things out of duty.

Answer: If one does not understand what they are doing and why they are doing it, then this may be considered mechanical. If one has no regrets and is satisfied with the neophyte position, then this is very likely to produce mechanical efforts. As long as the aspiring devotee is not complacent and is constantly trying to improve on the quality of their devotional service, then even though one may be doing many things out of duty, they will still make steady advancement.

Another case that will produce mechanical devotional service is when one understands what needs to be done, but basically executes their devotional service in a grudging mood. Such a person will also miss really connecting with the nectar of devotion. We have to remind ourselves that the execution of *bhakti* is not really so much what we do with our legs, hands or head. It has more to do with a focus on the heart. Therefore, even if we give our bodies

The Fourth Shower of Nectar

and our minds, our devotional service and our devotional consciousness will not fully mature unless we are simultaneously giving, or trying to give, our hearts.

Question: Sometimes it seems overwhelming trying to avoid all of the obstacles that we encounter in devotional service. There are so many, and they seem almost insurmountable. So how do we avoid becoming discouraged?

Answer: One does not have to worry about every *aparadha* and every single offense with such a detailed meditation. As with life in general, if we are so preoccupied with worrying about the things that we are trying to avoid, we will draw those things to us. We should also remind ourselves that Krishna Consciousness is less about things that we must stop, and more about doing the right thing. Proper actions and thoughts then begin to overtake our entire existence. Just as in the case of the *gosvamis*, they were not absorbed in what they had to avoid or minimize. Rather, they were so intensely absorbed with their *bhajana* that they would often forget to eat and to sleep.

Many years ago, when I was traveling with Satsvarupa Maharaja and Hridayananda Goswami, Srila Prabhupada sent a letter to us in reference to how we should preach at the universities. He explained that we should not go to the universities just preaching rules and regulations. We should explain to people how the Krishna conscious teachings are a higher philosophy. So, in other words, when someone can be informed about the benefits of something that is on a higher level, they will naturally be less likely to seek or stay with a lower scheme of things. We therefore do not want to pursue concerns that are unhealthy for us, but instead we want to keep the mind and all of the senses so occupied in connecting with and pursuing the higher, that we will have no time, energy or interest in associating with anything that is unhealthy for our spiritual progression.

If our minds feel too overwhelmed in trying to avoid what is inauspicious, we will become so depleted and distracted that we will miss many wonderful opportunities to pursue and connect with transcendence. After all, whatever we put most of our energy into is what we are bound to get more of in the future.

The Fifth Shower of Nectar

In the *Fifth Shower of Nectar*, Srila Visvanatha Cakravarti Thakura says, "The golden jewel of *bhakti* becomes more radiant when warmed in the fire of *abhyasa*, repeated devotional service, and this *abhyasa* conceives the taste for *bhakti* in the heart" (*Bhakti Trilogy*, 38). We just discussed how unmotivated and regulated actions move us faster towards our spiritual goal.

> "Ruci is defined as the taste or attraction that first helped the devotee to relish the process of hearing, and now ruci assists the devotee in the process of chanting. As the devotee's taste increases, the repetition of hearing and chanting seems not in the least exacting. Thereafter, ruci soon transforms into strong attachment for hearing and chanting. The devotee feels that any activities outside Krishna consciousness ones are a waste of energy."
>
> Bhakti Trilogy, 38

This means that as one begins to develop more taste for the spiritual, other enticements seem less and less attractive. "Gradually he begins to understand the import of the scriptures; this creates fresh interest for him and his studies are no longer a burden" (*Bhakti Trilogy*, 39). We first act mainly out of duty, which gradually begins to affect our speech and our consciousness. Then, after a while, it no longer seems like a chore—we begin to develop a taste for it. Later we begin to feel the positive effects of taking the nourishment. This is similar to taking medicine. When you are sick, the medicine or treatments may seem imposing at first. The medicine may even taste bitter. Nevertheless, you understand the benefits of the medicine, so you take it regularly despite the bitterness and adjust yourself to the prescription. Later, when you begin to see the benefits, you even become eager to take it.

Conditional Taste
Next he talks about two different types of *ruci* or two different levels of taste. First is *vastu vaisistya-apeksini*, which means special or specific requirements, or that which awaits specific requirements. The other category, called *vastu vaisistya-anapeksini*, does not await any requirements. *Vastu* means the object of worship—the Supreme Personality of Godhead. "In the first type of *ruci* certain requirements are desirable for hearing about Lord Krishna and chanting His name, form, qualities, pastimes and so on, in order for the devotee to

develop a taste for them" (*Bhakti Trilogy*, 39). In this case, a person will only perform their devotion with enthusiasm if certain requirements are there. They only want to hear the *bhajana* if someone has a professional or sweet voice. If someone plays the harmonium or tambora expertly, then they will eagerly hear and appreciate it. They can only appreciate visiting gorgeous temples and will only partake in a festival if hundreds and thousands of other people attend. Otherwise the festival will seem insignificant and they will not attend. They have many external attachments that they cannot move beyond.

This type of person is offensive because the individual's devotion is at a level where the external performance distracts them to the point that they may make offenses or speak harshly, without realizing that the quality of consciousness is much more important than expertise or skill. Instead of appreciating the devotee's offering to the Lord, they will think, "Why not let someone else sing?" Someone else may feel that they play the *mrdanga* expertly and can only play with another devotee who has the same expertise. Or the person will only play with a nice *kirtana* leader and actually put the *mrdanga* aside if someone else leads.

This type of *ruci* obviously will not attract Krishna very much despite the engagement in devotional activities. "We may ask the question that if a man is truly starving does he care about the quality or variety of food he is offered to eat?" (*Bhakti Trilogy*, 39) If someone really has greed to experience Krishna's higher mercy and blessings, external factors will not distract them. The presence of *vastu vaisistya-apeksini* indicates that a person is not worthy of receiving the higher blessings and is not sufficiently starving, because Krishna reciprocates based on the intensity of consciousness. If someone was really starving or hungry, would they really be so concerned about the details? Of course they would not have such discrimination.

Unconditional Taste

The second type of *ruci* is unlike the first type. A devotee who possesses this second type hears and chants the Lord's names, qualities and pastimes in a strong and steady way. The first type of *ruci* requires specific conditions such as a *kirtana* or *bhajana* with a beautiful melody. Srila Visvanatha Cakravarti Thakura explains the type of *ruci* that is independent of material considerations:

> *"Some of the symptoms of vastu vaisistya-anapeksini ruci are that the devotee thinks, 'Why have I foolishly exchanged the nectar of chanting Krishna's name for misfortune in the form of material life, hankering after what I do not possess and toiling to protect what I have gained. Despicable wretch that I am, I think of advising others! The causeless mercy*

of my spiritual master has delivered to me a priceless treasure, yet I could not value it. Instead, I chased after the mirage of material happiness. I wasted my life in a futile search for broken pieces of colored glass thinking them gems and so found myself in a fathomless ocean of materialism. I avoided all devotional activities and shamefully exhibited moral bankruptcy. Alas! I am bereft of any good character. My taste was such that I considered spurious talk valuable and tried in vain to relish it. Consequently I turned my back on the narrations of the transcendental qualities and names of the Supreme Lord. How great is my misfortune!"
Bhakti Trilogy, 40

In other words, the devotee has real hunger, recognizes his or her faults, and feels genuine regret and compunction that cleanses the devotee. He or she looks genuinely at their position, at the goal and at how to reach the goal. This type of mindset is conducive for advancement and acceleration. The devotee addresses the issues without denying them and has great intensity and greed; therefore, Krishna responds to their level of surrender.

"Thus in this way a devotee must

> repent. And someday, by a streak of good fortune, he will come across the greatest of all literatures, the works that describe the transcendental glories of the Supreme Personality of Godhead, Sri Gauranga. This literature captures the essence of the Vedas, which is said to be a mystical flowering tree fulfilling all desires. The devotee should become like a honey-bee who constantly drinks the ambrosia from the flower blossoms. Let the devotees seek the company of saints and shun the common crowds of money mongers. Residing in holy places, they must engage in serving the Supreme Lord with a pure heart."
>
> Bhakti Trilogy, 40-41

Keep in mind that as we move from the mechanical actions to the real enjoyment and experience, our taste increases and unfolds ultimately into *prema* or love of God.

Questions & Answers
Question: This discussion has helped me to reflect more deeply on appreciation. The other day I was on the altar performing an *arati* when a devotee started singing. To me, they sounded totally out of tune but I could do nothing about the situation. Then I realized that the offering is for Krishna's pleasure

and I am trying to enjoy His offering. Since I cannot enjoy it, I am criticizing it. Afterwards, I realized that I should not try to enjoy the Lord's offering. This is just another way to try to subtly enjoy something meant for Krishna's pleasure.

Answer: Yes, we should realize that it is much greater than just the external sound or the quality of sound—the important factor is the quality of consciousness. Sometimes people who sing the sweetest melodies are just performing for themselves. Once in Vrndavana, one of the devotees was a professional musician, had a very melodious voice, and played the instrument in the temple so wonderfully. Prabhupada later asked one of his servants, "Who is that *raksasa* singing down in the temple?" The devotee later fell down. Although he was very professional, he was thinking, "Everybody come and hear me. I am so wonderful and so beautiful." However, instead of honoring the sacredness of the environment and the Deity, he thought of himself as the Deity. His voice and performance were nice but a pure devotee was not impressed. Although the sound was seemingly pleasant, it lacked devotion. Devotion is most important.

Question: We have all heard of professional singers, and also those who professionally recite the *Bhagavatam* and *Ramayana*, but who often lack authentic devotion. How does one distinguish the genuine *bhakta* from the performer?

Answer: Of course, the most important thing is to become genuine ourselves. When we are fully absorbed in the authentic culture of *bhakti*, we will not be fooled or enticed by the pretenders or the offenders. We may even be able to have the potency to help such cheaters give up their pretense. If we cannot help them, at least they will not be able to have a negative impact on us. The more we are weak, doubtful or pretentious, the more we will be influenced and captivated by various cheaters and hypocrites. One way to see the difference between the genuine *bhakta* and the performer is that the performer is focusing on a particular delivery for a designated time. Therefore, even though the performer may seem genuine while delivering their message, if we study their character before or after their presentation, we will see inconsistencies. This is one of the traits of pretenders—they can never be fully consistent. The authentic *bhakta* is always fixed in glorifying Krishna and honoring *sastra*, whatever the environment may be. Such unalloyed devotees of the Lord see everything through the eyes of the scriptures, and therefore are eager to support taking full shelter of bona fide *sadhu, sastra* and *guru*. Because they have taken such legitimate shelter, their actions will also be legitimate. Pretenders, on the other hand, who have not really taken shelter of the scriptures, are more or less using the scriptures with ulterior motivations.

Question: Can you explain how, as one makes true

The Fith Shower of Nectar

advancement, it manifests as reduced attraction to any kind of sinful activity?

Answer: Material sense gratification and the culture of devotion do not go well together. One will cancel the other out. Where there is *jnana* and *vijnana* (knowledge and realized knowledge), nescience will be chased out. Just like with the previous answer, when someone is a pretender, we will later notice so much inconsistency. This will naturally be a sign that their consciousness is not fully absorbed in connecting with the higher truths. As we connect with the higher we will lose taste for the mundane. Attraction to the mundane is definitely a sign that the *bhakti* is not mature. When the *bhakti* is mature it will chase and kick out the lower alignments. We can evaluate someone not only by what they do, but also by what they do not do. The neophyte is mixed, but the *suddha-bhakta* is focused and consistent.

The conditioned soul is highly captured by lust. Lust blocks the flourishing of *prema*. When lust stands at the door, *prema* will not enter. When true *prema* is at the door, lust knows there is no room for facilitation or accommodation. True advancement is saying no to *kama* and yes to *prema*. However, *prema* will not come unless *nistha* (steadiness), *ruci* (taste), *asakti* (attachment) and *bhava* (spiritual emotion) set the stage or are a part of the welcoming party. If we genuinely want to become *suddha-bhaktas*, we must constantly absorb our minds and entire existence in authentic devotional culture, and in this way all that is inauspicious will be chased away to make room for that which is most auspicious—love and unalloyed service to the Divine Couple.

The Sixth Shower of Nectar

"As *ruci* ripens, the Supreme Personality of Godhead becomes the devotee's only object of worship and meditation. This is described as the stage of *asakti*, or attachment" (*Bhakti Trilogy*, 41).

> "*Asakti* is like a cluster of buds unfolding from the main stem of the creeper of devotion. Shortly, some of these buds may blossom into the flowers of *bhava*, or loving sentiments, and others may mature into the fruits of *prema*, or love of Godhead." (*Bhakti Trilogy*, 41)
>
> "In that case we can conclude that the difference between *ruci* and *asakti* lies in how mature is the devotee's confidential meditation."
>
> *Bhakti Trilogy*, 42

The quality of the mental *bhajana* and mental absorption depends on how deep the inner life progresses and how much one begins to address their spiritual aspect rather than the mere physical.

It depends on their readiness to tune into their *sanatana* nature, their hunger for reinstatement in the spiritual kingdom, their hunger to know their ultimate relationship with Krishna, and their hunger to reflect on the great saints, *sadhus* and *acaryas*. Although these great *acaryas* may not be physically with us anymore in this universe, one's acceleration to the next level also depends on how much one identifies with them and prays to them. One who thinks of the saints as part of ancient history or feels an inability to access their mercy will be far from them. If we think that the great saints such as Madhvacarya, Ramanujacarya, Jiva Goswami, Mukunda dasa, Raghunatha Bhatta Goswami, Srila Visvanatha Cakravarti, Jesus or Muhammad have departed and left us to struggle on our own, they will always remain far from us. If we relish the activities of these saints as if they just happened this morning and try to truly connect with the *acaryas* in this mood, then we will speed up our progress. The *acaryas* have come to help reclaim all living entities. We should not just engage in some performance, or worship them in lofty ways, but we should connect deeply with them. Strong attachment, *asakti*, gradually transforms into *bhava*, or devotional service in ecstasy at which point we begin to experience effects on our speech and bodies based on the love of God that begins to penetrate our consciousness.

Questions & Answers
Question: How do we deepen our mental *bhajana*?

The Sixth Shower of Nectar

Answer: Practically everything that we do in devotional service is to strengthen our mental *bhajana*, or internal absorption with our real identity as eternal servants of Krishna. As we improve the quality of following the ninefold process—*sravana* (hearing), *kirtana* (chanting), *visnoh smarana* (remembering), *pada-sevana* (worshiping the Lord's lotus feet), *arcana* (worshiping the Deity), *vandana* (prayer), *dasya* (becoming the servant), *sakhya* (becoming the friend) and *atma-nivedana* (surrendering everything)—we deepen our mental *bhajana*. We all have so much internal dialogue throughout the day. For most people, over 80% of their internal dialogue is negative. We are far more a product of what we think than of what we say and do, for our thoughts dictate our actions and arrange our futures. We need to exercise care in harnessing the mind. A mind that is uncontrolled will not be able to engage in deep *bhajana*. As we focus more on Krishna's and the great *acarya's nama* (name), *rupa* (form), *guna* (qualities) and *lila* (pastimes), the mind will become naturally intoxicated with the higher *bhakti*, and this will produce a rich state of Krishna consciousness.

Question: When I reflect on the many great *acaryas* that we are connected with, it gives me such wonderful solace, but can you explain how we can access even more of their mercy?

Answer: Once again this draws our attention to our mental culture. *Vandana* (prayer) is extremely important. We should constantly pray to our spiritual masters and to the great *acaryas* in our line. After all, they are working as a team and they are all concerned about our success. When we do something that is proper, we get the blessings of the *parampara* chain of great spiritual mentors. The more we are able to realize how much help and facilitation is available, the more alert we will be to take advantage of the help. So often, we do not get proper assistance because we are not aware of what is available, nor sufficiently eager to take advantage of opportunity. As we pray to our *acaryas* and mentors, we connect with them in a deep part of our psyche. This way we not only get their blessings, but also their guidance and protection. One common difficulty is how we allow time and space to be a source of interference. Time and space in the material world have a powerful way of producing separation and fragmentation, but we have to remind ourselves that these great personalities' love and guidance is not limited or restricted by material phenomena. Although we do not physically see them, connecting with them is always possible when we open ourselves up to receive their transmissions. They are always sending guidance, love and protection. Unfortunately, most of us work overtime in finding ways to avoid and ignore them. It is also important that we remind ourselves that it is our natural position to be in pure association with Krishna and His divine agents. Therefore, our focus is on trying to give up all of our unhealthy acculturation. We want to give up the *ruci*, or the taste, for the mundane by once again tasting the sublime. These great *acaryas* have come to teach us by their own example what it means to experience and live with the highest devotional emotions. They are sending us a wakeup call to come to join them.

Reflections on Sacred Teachings, Volume Two

The Seventh Shower of Nectar

> *"The sweet, far-reaching fragrance of the blossoms of bhava sends enchanting invitations to the Supreme Lord, gently inducing Him to appear in person before His devotee."*
> *Bhakti Trilogy, 45*

As we connect more with this great legacy and with our inner existence, we will have more greed and hunger, which will summon Krishna and His eternal servants. It is comparable to an e-mail message or a fax line that makes a connection and induces the Lord to appear before the devotee. This call goes directly to the Lord and induces Him to connect with and even personally appear before His very hungry servants.

> *"Furthermore, when the soul's natural sentiments are even faintly scented by bhava, they melt and flow unrestrained toward the Supreme Lord, bathing His divine form with*

> *love...Bhava is self-willed and moves on its own volition."*
> *Bhakti Trilogy, 45*

As we mentioned earlier, *bhakti* is not just relegated to ritual, to knowledge, or to any external condition.

Sublime Meditation

> *"The actions of a devotee in bhava are unpredictable—he may suddenly try to imagine how it feels to be touched by the tender palms of the Lord, and when all the hairs of his body stand on end, it appears as if it is actually happening to him."*
> *Bhakti Trilogy, 45*

Once a devotee has reached this platform of *bhava* and deeply entered the powerful taste of love of God, he or she begins to experience amazing transformations. At first, it is more of a mental *bhajana* but, as the devotee thinks deeply of the Lord, then the Lord reciprocates to the point that He actually appears before His devotee.

> *"On other occasions the devotee's nostrils flare from inhaling deeply the sweet lingering aroma of the Lord's transcendental body, sending him*

The Seventh Shower of Nectar

into raptures. Sometimes he thinks, 'Shall I ever be fortunate enough to relish the ambrosia issuing from Krishna's sublime lips?' Immediately he begins to lick his own lips as if his taste buds have been given a magnificent treat only his cherished dream could fulfill. Again at times such a devotee experiences waves of pleasure transmitted from the Lord, the reservoir of all pleasures, and an ineffable joy envelops his heart, making him feel the same as when he sees the Lord face-to-face."
Bhakti Trilogy, 45-46)

"In *bhava-bhakti*, the devotee focuses his mind with unwavering attention on the Supreme Lord. In sleeping, waking or dreaming he always remembers Krishna" (*Bhakti Trilogy*, 46). Now the devotion becomes an internal *bhajana* while in the waking state, the sleeping state and the dream state. Being in the physical body is comparable to a state of amnesia in which we have forgotten our identity and higher nature. The devotee slowly begins to recover from this unfortunate state. In *bhajana* and reflections, the devotee begins to think extensively about Krishna's pastimes and begins to imagine touching, hearing or smelling the Lord. In this meditative state, the devotee begins to experience the transcendental *bhava* or ecstasy as if it has begun to happen completely.

This gradually grades into *prema*, in which the experience distinctly happens and becomes the devotee's full identity. The devotee's intense *laulya* or greed is an intense call to Krishna. Consequently, Krishna and His divine agents begin to reciprocate to such an extent that the devotee becomes less and less of a physical entity. Although remaining in his or her physical body, their original *svarupa* comes forth and begins to manifest, and the devotee begins to live more on the inside than on the outside. The devotee begins to live in the internal realm and experience reciprocation based on more than the external. This occurs not only to *Vaisnavas* but also to some very advanced saints who talk about being in love with God. Many times they will literally enter a state of trance and ecstasy based on the activities in the internal realm.

Devotional Trance

Srila Prabhupada explains that when a very advanced devotee goes into trance, he often separates from the physical realm temporarily and enters into the spiritual realm just as a person can put a coat aside and later return for it. The stimulation from these experiences is of such a high nature that the devotee's present existence cannot contain it; therefore, the "coat" must be put down temporarily in order to become fully absorbed in the experience. For example, when Madhavendra Puri saw a black cloud, he thought of Krishna as blackish Syamasundara, causing him to go into a trance. His

The Seventh Shower of Nectar

true "self" identified with the experience, but his temporary identity could not contain the experience. Consequently, the temporary identity had to be put aside but it later returned. Devotees will sometimes seem to be crazy because they do not relate to the "normal" scheme of life. They may even go days and days without any desire to eat or sleep, or they may respond mechanically to these temporary stimuli. Their higher pleasures and realizations are causing them to lose attraction for the mundane realms and activities.

A more advanced devotee, an *uttama-adhikari*, will step down in order to relate better to the environment and to the duality, and to process the environment as others process it. Otherwise, if the *uttama-adhikari* always acted according to their normal feelings, they would seem like a mad person or seem to be suffering from an epileptic seizure. When they heard anything about the Lord, they would immediately cry, jump, shout or fall over due to the intensity of *prema*. They would not even be able to preach because they would not see the difference between the atheists and the theists. They would not see some people as inimical and others as favorable because they would only see the true essence of every person. It would be impossible to preach if they did not see the patterns that need adjustment. So, they come down temporarily to assist and deal with the temporary external relative affairs. However, if someone imbibes this *bhava*, it is as if they are moving into a whole different identity. They are less and less distracted by duality or the modes of material nature.

> *"In sleeping, waking or dreaming he always remembers Krishna. With incessant and intense desire to properly serve the Lord, the devotee in bhava discovers his original spiritual form. Naturally and perfectly gliding into that form, he more or less discards his sadhaka tabernacle."*
> Bhakti Trilogy, 46

As the devotee undergoes these experiences, he or she gradually accepts their identity, begins to have pastimes on that level and begins to connect with eternal associates.

Revealing Bhava

> *"This bhava is of two kinds: raga-bhakti-uttha (springing from spontaneous devotional service) and vaidha-bhakti-uttha (springing from regulated devotional service). A devotee displaying the first kind of bhava (raga-bhakti-uttha) denounces worship in awe and reverence because he shies away from any awareness of position (jati) and*

The Seventh Shower of Nectar

scriptural knowledge and edicts (pramana)."

Bhakti Trilogy, 46

A person in this spontaneous mood no longer has as much attachment to the rules and regulations. *The Nectar of Devotion* explains that when a person acquires this mood, they still remain in a kind of teaching position and still have to deal externally with other people; therefore, they continue to act as if they have not attained it because it would cause confusion. For instance, Srila Prabhupada would chant rounds and engage in many different services although he did not have to. The idea is how to encourage and facilitate others so that they can continue gradually in their devotional service. This is one of the factors that distinguish genuine devotees from *Sahajiyas* because, if someone reaches this level, they are not supposed to display it publicly and create a disturbance. A public display causes people to become more fascinated with some of the symptoms and expressions than with the development of internal consciousness. These displays also cause people who have not done the proper cleansing to act falsely, hoping to gain respect and honor. Consequently, there will be confusion about the existence of real *bhakti* and the real symptoms of love of Godhead. In order to avoid such confusion and disturbances, it is recommended that those who have attained this stage should not externally act upon it. However, when people at this level are together or are in touch with someone of that higher nature, it is not necessary to try to be diplomatic or to worry about harming others in the environment. These greatly evolved souls mercifully check themselves externally to avoid causing immature people, who are not ready to actually decrease their involvement with material nature, to hurt their devotional creeper by acting falsely. They want them to act properly in order to pay the dues necessary to later experience that which is available. But once these souls are among themselves, as in the nighttime *kirtana* that was held at Srivasa Thakura's house, they do not have any restrictions because all the personalities present are evolved beings and their expressions are of a high caliber.

When Srila Prabhupada associated with his very exalted godbrothers, you would see a different mood of exchange. At times, Prabhupada would meet one of these godbrothers and they would act almost like children. They would talk in their language and act giddy and childlike. Once in Vrndavana, a tattered *sadhu* was trying to see Srila Prabhupada in his room. He said, "I want to see your Prabhupada." The guard wanted to keep the *sadhu* at a distance, thinking that too many people wanted to see the *guru*, as in a zoo. One day while he was not on guard, he noticed that this very tattered *babaji* snuck in. When the *sadhu* entered, he and Prabhupada both hit the floor offering obeisances, embraced each other and began interacting like children. They were in a childish mood similar to the mood of cowherd boys and were talking in a giddy, humorous way. When the guard saw this, he felt very embarrassed, realizing that he had offended this seemingly ordinary *sadhu* who was actually an exalted soul.

The idea is to follow the process with dedication and determination. Some of our engagements may not enthuse us much in the beginning, just as bitter medicine may not appeal to us initially but, as we begin to see the positive effects, we will start taking it without a sense of anxiety. Later we will even begin to relish it because of the benefits that become a part of our being. In our devotion, we receive guidance from *sadhu*, *sastra* and *guru*—as we honor the guidance in the right way and remove the blocks and obstacles, gradually our experiences move from the physical level to the spiritual. We discussed the importance of speaking more about the philosophy as well as reflecting on it and sharing it with others. As we begin to reflect on our devotion more and develop a higher taste, *param drstva nivartate*, many of the other problems that produce anxiety and frustration are put to the side. Now the divinity begins to come forth and we begin to rediscover our natural inherent treasures that we have somehow forsaken.

Questions & Answers

Question: It seems that the lifestyle of a devotee is not geared to the internal but rather it is more geared to the external due to the many services involved. I find that, in household life, my only quiet time is around midnight and by that time I feel so exhausted that all I can think about is sleep. It reminds me of the book *Chota's Way* by Satsvarupa dasa Goswami. Chota wanted to spend more time reading and chanting but his associates wanted him to preach and deal with administration. How do we balance the need to be active in our services with the need to connect internally?

Answer: Srila Prabhupada explains that there is nothing wrong if one is able go to Vrndavana and chant all day long; however, few people can do that. Since most people are unable to be satisfied with only chanting and praying, we need different engagements to help us develop that rich, internal connection. Furthermore, we are not *bhajananandis* but we are *gosthy-anandis.* Therefore, we are not just interested in *moksa* or salvation but we are interested in growing and developing in order to serve and facilitate. This is the mood of Mahaprabhu. It is not the mood of trying to engage in *dharma*, rituals, piety, economic development, *moksa* or self-realization for our own well-being. Instead, the devotee sincerely tries to grow in order to increase their service, which means activity and interaction if we have the capacity. Although circumstances such as health may prevent such interaction, we should always try to internally grow so that we can somehow serve Srila Prabhupada's mission and humanity.

We can still develop the internal while we are physically active by reminding ourselves about what

The Seventh Shower of Nectar

we are doing and why we are doing it. It is important to constantly reflect on the philosophy connected with our engagements. The majority of Srila Prabhupada's servants who fell down were those who were not reading constantly. Without the philosophy, a person will see the service simply as work. They would begin to see Srila Prabhupada as just an elderly prophet who needs assistance and they would develop an offensive mentality. However, if we serve with humility and remain fearful of the crazy mind, the unhealthy mindset can be replaced by constant remembrance of the *sastra*. Then we will be able to develop a certain level of stability in order to avoid some of the pitfalls associated with such. Both the internal and external engagements are needed. We need socialization and physical stimulation to assist in proper talking and thinking, and we need proper thinking to help us to act in the proper way.

Question: I recently read a pastime from the *Radha-Damodara Vilasa* by Vaiyasaki dasa. It was explained in the book that Radharani is so attracted by the pastime of Mother Yasoda binding Krishna with a rope that she also wants to attract Krishna in this way. Therefore, she performs a *vrata*. I did not fully understand the *vrata* although it is called the *Katyayani-vrata*. I could not find any more information on this *vrata* and was hoping that you could expound on this topic.

Answer: This particular *lila* in which Mother Yasoda

binds Krishna with the rope of her love is so attractive to Srimati Radharani because She also wants to capture Krishna in this way. In the *lila*, there is this constant togetherness, separation and even mischievousness. Radharani is absorbed and appreciating that Mother Yasoda has captured Krishna in such a way and He is fully under her control. Sometimes Radharani and the *manjaris* worship the goddess or demigod, which may confuse us because we do not worship demigods. However, we can worship demigods to ask them to help us become better servants of Krishna. In this case, although the *puja* or worship is executed, it is in the mood of trying to offer more to Krishna. We are not oblivious to the *devas*. Sometimes a neophyte devotee may blaspheme Jesus or Buddha while preaching—this is very unhealthy and is not in line with our philosophy. The *devas* and demigods are agents of Krishna and they have their activities and missions. However, in the process of *bhakti*, we try to dive deep into *prema* and engage in necessary activities on this path toward eternal association with the Lord. Therefore, we honor these personalities but do not get distracted.

For example, in the process of considering several people to write a foreword for one of our books, we contacted the President of Nigeria. After the request was made I tried to find out the level of progress. My request had gone to one of his ministers and later it would go to the President. We needed to connect with the ministers because they have a specific role in relation to the President and they could ensure that the President did the foreword. We could not offend the ministers and expect to reach the President, because they could also block or interfere with our ability to connect. At the same time, we did not want the ministers to write the foreword, we wanted the President. So, we made an appeal to the minister to see that the President returned the foreword to us in a timely fashion. Similarly, the devotee can make some connection with the demigods but it should be done with a higher goal in mind.

Eighth Shower of Nectar

Prema is ultimately our most natural and healthy position. At this point, we are becoming more and more sane and less affected by the amnesia. It is comparable to a person's recovery from a chronic disease in which they gradually become more stable and eventually regain their health. The real natural position of every living entity is the total intoxication of being completely in love. Our entire experience is based on the highest expression of love and on fully receiving Krishna's highest offering and association of love. Srila Visvanatha Cakravarti ends this *Madhurya-Kadambini* with these discussions of *prema*. This *Eighth Shower of Nectar* concludes the *Madhurya- Kadambini*.

> "Alongside the blossoming of prema, marvelous changes occur. The devotee's consciousness, previously entrapped by materialistic attachments for home and family, is now inspired by prema to disdainfully discard them and set itself free."
> Bhakti Trilogy, 48

In endless lifetimes, the devotee has accepted identities as a man, a woman, a king, a queen, a demigod, a *gandharva* or even a *raksasa*. In each case, the individual received an abode, an arrangement or various types of facilities to work out certain issues, but they ultimately looked for *prema* in all the wrong directions.

Developing Desire

> *"Just as the touchstone jewel transforms ordinary objects to gems by touching them, by its potency prema also miraculously transforms earthly attachments and makes them shine with sublime resplendence like its own self. Prema enfolds these attachments and bathes them in the nectar of the Supreme Lord's transcendental name, beauty, qualities, and so on."*
>
> Bhakti Trilogy, 48

"The pure devotee thus begins to desire at every moment a direct audience with the Lord" (*Bhakti Trilogy*, 49). We understand that we should never ask Krishna for anything beside service. However, the pure devotee at this level feels unqualified but is asking, demanding and begging for that audience in order to serve the Lord in variegated ways. In relation to *bhava* as described in the previous chapter,

The Eighth Shower of Nectar

each sense is becoming alive and excited after being dead for so many, many lifetimes. They are becoming excited to be in touch with different aspects of the spiritual world and Krishna's association. Then the devotee becomes mad.

> *"The burning arrow of extreme eagerness lacerates him, its intensity causing him dissatisfaction despite his exulting in the Supreme Lord's sublime beauty and ambrosial pastimes...The exultation of a devotee experiencing prema is likened to a traveler who, after painfully traversing the burning desert sand in the middle of summer, finds an oasis cooled by a fresh stream gurgling under the shade of a huge banyan tree."*
>
> *Bhakti Trilogy, 49*

This experience is comparable to a traveler who has been in the sandy desert and dying of thirst and hunger. The person is desperately wandering about having hallucinations of water, having flashbacks of the past, thinking of the future or meditating on their relationships. The traveler might be thinking about what he or she could have done or did not do while experiencing such anxiety and anticipation for the food and drink. So Srila Visvanatha Cakravarti Thakura is describing the position of the living entity in the conditioned state who is a sleep walker and is more dead than alive. Here the person in the desert is almost dead and is barely maintaining his life air when he comes upon food and water. He is describing the intake of *prema* in this way.

> *"The bliss of prema is further likened to the happiness a wild elephant feels after being trapped for days in a smoldering forest fire and then suddenly drenched in torrential rains..."*
>
> Bhakti Trilogy, 49-50

Imagine a large, wild elephant in the middle of an intense fire that sometimes burns his body. He is in a crazed state, struggling for life, when all of a sudden tremendous torrents of rain fall and extinguish the fire. Similarly, our body is on fire due to excessive sense gratification, fear, lust, anger, enviousness and intoxication. All of these disturbances result from our own mind. We constantly suffer from the threefold miseries which are *adhyatmika, adhidaivika* and *adhibhautika* or disturbances from our own mind, disturbances from the *devas* or the environment, and disturbances from other living entities. We have been subjected to all of these sufferings while undergoing *samsara* but, all of a sudden, it just becomes part of the past. It is as if we simply walk through a door from one room into another and these miseries no longer disturb or haunt us.

"...Or like a gourmet, who after many days of sickness and being fed medicines and a bland, frugal diet becomes well and is given a feast" (*Bhakti Trilogy*, 50). Many know the feeling of diving into a huge feast after a fast, a sickness or an austere diet.

> *"Of course, these descriptions offer merely an idea of the devotee's state of joy because it cannot be compared to any material happiness. Material happiness and spiritual happiness are totally different from each other by nature..."*
>
> Bhakti Trilogy, 50

He gives us various examples or analogies to help us understand the idea of moving from one situation to the next in a mood of great desperation that later turns to great fulfillment, satiation and satisfaction.

An Audience with the Lord

Now Srila Visvanatha Cakravarti gives the stages or experiences that begin to manifest due to the presence of *prema*. First the Lord reveals His form of matchless beauty to the enraptured devotee and personally appears. "The devotee's senses and mind become one and he beholds with all his senses the Lord's exquisite beauty" (*Bhakti Trilogy*, 50). In the spiritual body, one sense can perform the activities of all the other senses. Here the devotee is regaining his or her complete spiritual body and, while viewing the Lord in *prema*, all of the senses come together or converge in order to observe the Lord. It is not that the eyes alone are absorbing the Lord but all the senses are connecting with the eyes to behold the beauty of His form. The mind also converges.

> *"At the sight of the Lord's unparalleled beauty, the devotee feels ecstatic symptoms (asta-sattvic vikara) like being paralyzed, quivering, weeping and so on. These ecstatic symptoms begin to hinder his vision of the Lord; not only that, but the exhilaration renders him unconscious."*
>
> *Bhakti Trilogy, 50*

So all of the senses are converging. This occurs after the devotee develops such *laulya* or greed. The intense greed manifests after the devotee follows the process with great effort and mercy. Now he or she is receiving benedictions and is awakening from the amnesia. Any previous desires have now converged into the single desire of only wanting to be with the Lord and His associates; therefore, the Lord reciprocates and sends a message. Under the mercy of Srimati Radharani, the Mother of Devotion, the soul has now been fully noticed and has fully noticed the Lord because the Lord is always present and available. So first is the sight perception. It involves more than just the eyes because all of the senses also rush

The Eighth Shower of Nectar

to make the connection. All the senses including the mind rush and converge to make this overwhelming contact, rendering the devotee unconscious.

> *"Seeing the devotee's condition, the Lord consolingly manifests His second ambrosial attribute– His physical fragrance–which immediately arrests the devotee's sense of smell. Now all the devotee's senses withdraw from the sense of sight and rush to center on the sense of smell."*
>
> Bhakti Trilogy, 50

First the devotee gazes upon the Lord's magnificent form and then the Lord allows His sensational aroma to revitalize the devotee. Next, all the senses rush to the sense of smell. "This overpowers him, and once again intense joy causes him to lose consciousness" (*Bhakti Trilogy*, 50). This is unbelievable. Who would want material sense gratification when such opportunities are available? "Krishna once again rescues the devotee, and this time the Lord revives him with His melodious voice" (*Bhakti Trilogy*, 50). The devotee first sees the Lord's form, the senses all rush there and he goes unconscious. Then the Lord wakes him with the ambrosial fragrance from His body, from the sandalwood and the flowers. That sweetness then revives the devotee and the senses rush there in full consciousness. The devotee becomes entirely absorbed in experiencing more of the Lord and again falls unconscious.

> "The Lord speaks to him saying, 'My dear devotee! I am now your captive, fully under your control. Do not be overwhelmed, just perceive Me and fulfill the desire of your heart.' The devotee's senses become surcharged and they seek to hear and absorb the sweet melody of his beloved Lord's voice."
> Bhakti Trilogy, 50

Krishna sees the devotee's state, revives him and gives His association in various ways, and the devotee loses consciousness after each experience.

> "The devotee's senses become surcharged and they seek to hear and absorb the sweet melody of his beloved Lord's voice. Again he is unable to contain his ecstasy and he becomes bereft of consciousness."
> Bhakti Trilogy, 50

Just hearing the Lord speak such words, the devotee becomes totally unconscious.

> "Then the Lord, full of compassion, embraces the devotee with His body,

displaying His fourth nectarean opulence of tender youthfulness. To the dasya devotee, (mellow of servitorship) He places His lotus feet on his head; to the sakhya devotee (mellow of friendship) He entwines His lotus fingers with his fingers; to the vatsalya devotee (parental mellow) the Lord wipes away his tears with His lotus hands; and to the madhurya devotee (conjugal mellow) He draws him to His chest and wraps His arms around him in a tender embrace. From this we understand that the Lord reciprocates appropriately with the different mellows of each devotee's love.

"Just as before, when the devotee swoons in indescribable joy, the Lord shows His fifth opulence, that of versatile loving exchanges. Krishna offers the devotee sublime ambrosia in the form of chewed remnants from His mouth and lips. As the bhakta fully relishes it, his sense of taste becomes satiated. At this stage the Lord appears to His devotee who is now absorbed in the conjugal mellow, and initiates him into a transcendental emotional exchange of intense loving intimacy, long

> *coveted by him. Of course, the Lord never divulges such a confidential mood to any other devotee except one who is in madhurya-rasa (conjugal mellow)."*
>
> *Bhakti Trilogy, 50-51*

We see that no mellow is excluded. According to the way in which the entity wants to eternally be with the Lord, the Lord receives him or her and inaugurates them into their eternal activities and exchanges.

> *"Once again the devotee is drawn into an overwhelming mood of divine bliss from this intimate encounter with the Lord, and again he swoons. The Lord's succor to him this time is in the form of showers of audarya, or magnanimity—His sixth transcendental attribute. In this condition the devotee will not respond to any consoling. Audarya in this instance means when all the transcendental attributes of the Lord are at one time forced onto the devotee's conglomerate senses: sight, hearing, mind. Prema now responds almost as if to the Lord's bidding. It waxes by leaps and bounds, and*

The Eighth Shower of Nectar

> *the devotee's thirst for it increases proportionately. Gradually, like the waxing moon, these transcendental attributes combine together to mature fully. Uncountable like the waves in the ocean of unlimited bliss, a plethora of transcendental pastimes helps prema to stir and shatter the devotee's heart. Prema then installs itself in the devotee's mind as its guardian deity, repairing and rebuilding his inner being. Prema radiates its energy, audarya, in such a way that the devotee is able to relish unhindered all of the Lord's transcendental qualities."*
>
> *Bhakti Trilogy, 51*

This means that first they are coming through the different senses. The devotee feels overwhelmed when the Lord reciprocates but the Lord revives the devotee again and again. Then the Lord embraces and involves the devotee in transcendental activities. Now the Lord is giving this intense mercy so that the experiences are no longer just coming in flashes but they are installed within the devotee's full existence and consciousness. In other words, all of this eternally occurs simultaneously.

> *"Thus it cannot be refuted that the devotee can taste to his complete*

> *satisfaction all the different qualities of the Lord, nor can it be argued that he relishes full bliss at this stage... The pure devotee is eager to relish altogether each of the Lord's sublime attributes such as His exquisite beauty. But just as a swallow with its beak shut tight is unable to slake its thirst even when it rains, so the devotee is also helpless on his own against the Lord's opulences inundating his senses. Seeing the devotee's predicament the Lord thinks, 'Is this confusion the purpose of My matchless beauty?' So the Lord offers to the devotee His seventh opulence, compassion. This opulence is the headmistress of all other attributes."*
>
> *Bhakti Trilogy, 51-52*

Krishna has given Himself fully and the devotee is experiencing this overwhelming position due to the intense love that they are sharing. Now Krishna is making additional arrangements for this devotee's eternal existence of relishing the mellows.

"This seventh opulence of the Lord is also known as *anugraha*, or mercy. She manifests herself in the Lord's lotus eyes in varied splendor" (*Bhakti Trilogy*, 52). Now Srila Visvanatha is explaining how this level of compassion is given and how it is experienced in different *rasas*.

> "To the dasya-bhakta she is compassion, to the vatsalya-bhakta she is filial fondness, and to the madhurya-bhakta she is heart-melting magnetic power. In this way she appears in many forms matching the different loving moods of the devotees."
>
> *Bhakti Trilogy, 52*

Overcoming Our Disqualifications

> "The scriptures have identified eighteen human shortcomings that go against its tenets. They are as follows: illusion, sleepiness, uncivility, lust, greed, madness, envy, cruelty, lamentations, over-endeavor, deceit, anger, desire, fear, mistakes, intolerance and dependence."
>
> *Bhakti Trilogy, 53*

In other words, these are the obstacles that have prevented the living entity from participating in all these available experiences. As we quickly throw these blocks away, we then have a chance to be freed of the amnesia. For this reason Srila Visvanatha began by first explaining stagnations such as the enemies of the mind, the distractions and the different types of *anarthas*.

"The scriptures proclaim that the Lord's qualities are absolutely free from these discrepancies" (*Bhakti Trilogy,* 53). People normally think that they will become happy by doing what they want, when they want and how they want; however, it is the opposite. The more people continue to put themselves in anxiety with their envy, lust, greed, fear and doubt, the more they simply maintain the physical body along with all of its bombardments and frustrations. Ultimately this leads to sickness and death. For this reason, devotional service is based on the intensity of taking shelter of humility, simplicity, surrender and unmotivated, unconditional service. It is really based on how to receive everything by giving up everything. As we give up all material attachments, we make ourselves available to receive all spiritual blessings.

However, the living entity thinks, "No, I cannot give this up. I must have it." Or the entity thinks, "Krishna, You want me to give up everything. Well, first You give." But the burden is on us. We have been the criminals. A criminal may demand freedom from prison, claiming they have been reformed, but the burden is on them. They have been acting improperly and they have the responsibility to show how they have changed. The warden will not release them with the blind hopes that they will change. Similarly, we do not return without acting according to our eternal position in the spiritual world. This will show our readiness to be freed from these shackles. It is not that when you leave the body,

The Eighth Shower of Nectar

you automatically return to the spiritual world due to some undue mercy. First you must become like the spiritual world. First the senses and the body must be transcendentally absorbed, which will then lead to the verbal absorption. Next the mental level will settle in stronger and stronger. Then the other contaminations will fall to the background. In most cases, our body is not properly absorbed in spiritual associations and, if the speech is mundane, the mind will just be about *aham mameti*. "I want this for myself. I will stop this engagement because it inconveniences me. I do not like this activity or that one." This becomes the mental absorption, and will not produce the unconditional, unmotivated loving body that Krishna will fully associate with; rather, it will produce or reinforce more of the physical body that falls under the attacks of the enemies of the mind.

> *"The Supreme Lord acknowledges His devotee's feelings and says to him, 'My dear devotee, you have sacrificed wife, children, wealth and home countless times in many births. You have tolerated such sufferings as the ravages of scorching summers, freezing winters, hunger, thirst, pain and disease only so you could serve Me as I had asked you to. You have disregarded a million humiliations from others and maintained your life*

> *by begging, yet so far I have been unable to reciprocate with you and offer you anything. This makes Me indebted to you. Now tell Me, what can I offer you? Lordship of the entire universe, the position of Lord Brahma, all the mystic opulences, and so on are not befitting, hence how can I offer them to you? Is it becoming of a gentleman to offer grass, straw and other animal fodder to a human being? Considering all this, I offer Myself to you; although I am unconquerable and indomitable, I am won over by you—I am now your property."*
>
> *Bhakti Trilogy, 53*

The Lord knows the sacrifices that His devotees make lifetime after lifetime. Krishna is not speaking to those who have not made such sacrifices and who are not ready for such because these are the necessary qualifications. One becomes all for Krishna and offers everything to Him. Krishna says that, because the devotee has done so much for Him and consequently come to this level, the devotee can now receive Him in full. Krishna says that He has watched His devotee tolerate such struggles for so many lifetimes and now He cannot repay the devotee. The Lord says, "What can I repay you with? The position of Lord Brahma or some other demigod is not enough. Maybe I could give you lordship over universes? No, this is not sufficient. Mystical opulences? No. It is belittling to think that after you have persevered lifetime after lifetime, I will only give you such insignificant boons. Well, I will have to give you Myself."

> *"'Considering all this, I offer Myself to you; although I am unconquerable and indomitable, I am won over by you—I am now your property. I shall simply depend on your gentle disposition.' The Lord's ambrosial words enter the devotee's ears like pearly drops of nectar. The devotee replies, 'My dear Lord! O Supreme Person! You are an ocean of mercy. Seeing me swept away by the swift currents of gross materialism and becoming the helpless prey of the cruel venomous snake of Time, You took pity on me. Your petal-soft heart melted, and to remove my lust and nescience You appeared before me as the most perfect spiritual preceptor. Your appearance is awe-inspiring, like the powerful presence of the Sudarsana Cakra is to His natural enemies, You thus rescued me from the horrendous poisonous fangs and grim black coils of the snake of Time.'"*
> Bhakti Trilogy, 53-54

Qualifications of a Pure Devotee

When the devotee speaks, a competition begins between the Lord and His servant.

> "'Your intention is to elevate me to become Your maidservant so I can serve Your divine lotus feet, and so You have made Yourself available in the form of the most purifying of syllables—Your holy names—which are nondifferent from You. Your holy names enter my ears and alleviate my excruciating pain, allowing me to repeatedly hear, chant and remember Your transcendental names and pastimes. You are reforming me. Although you have kindly placed me in the assembly of Your pure eternal associates and taught the process of surrender to You, I am so flagitious and fallen that I did not serve You even for a moment. I am fit to be severely rebuked for this atrocious act. Yet You spared me and instead made my eyes drink the most sublime vision—that of Your beatific face. And still You say, 'Now I am indebted to you?'"
>
> Bhakti Trilogy, 54

> "'These words spoken by my beloved Lord have deeply disturbed

> me. At this juncture I am thinking about my next course of action. To ask to be pardoned for the sins of a few lifetimes, nay a million lifetimes, would be audacious on my part. In fact I feel my wicked offences number more than trillions and have been accumulating since time immemorial. I have already suffered some of their consequences and whatever is left, let me face them, for I refuse to beg for them to be absolved.'"
> Bhakti Trilogy, 54

The devotee's level of humility is so high that, even after attaining this height, he feels unworthy in this loving, verbal exchange.

> "These words of endless remorse and lamentation flow freely from the devotee. This pleases the Lord immensely. The Lord reciprocates with the preyasi mood, the mood of a stricken beloved for her lover, which these elevated devotees exhibit. He fulfills their yearnings and immediately manifests Vrndavana, the land immortalized for staging His transcendental pastimes. There the devotee sees Krishna with His most beloved gopi, Srimati Radharani,

> *daughter of King Vrsabhanu."*
> *Bhakti Trilogy, 55*

Then after all of these exchanges Krishna, due to His higher level of compassion and feelings of exhilaration due the devotee's love, manifests Vrndavana for the living entity. Then the devotee witnesses the many exchanges taking place in that eternal *rasa*.

> *"Thereafter, the devotee becomes more or less aware of himself and his immediate surroundings. His eyes flutter open and, finding that his beloved Lord is nowhere to be seen, he begins to pine for Him. Unrestrained tears pour down his cheeks in streams."*
> *Bhakti Trilogy, 56*

Remember that the devotee is still in the physical body.

> *"He ponders, 'Was I in a dream? No, if it were so I would be still drowsy and my eyes would be sticky from sleep. Then was it all created by someone's mystic powers? That is also not plausible, because the bliss I experienced is not an illusion or something mundane. Maybe it was a hallucination, an error of the mind. That is also not true, otherwise I*

The Eighth Shower of Nectar

> *would feel restless and my heart empty. Could it be all a fabrication of a fertile imagination? No, this experience is beyond the capacity of any imagination. The other possibility is that the Lord's vision may suddenly appear in the mind's eye because of extreme happiness. This is also ruled out because on every previous occasion when I saw the Lord I can remember what they were like, but my present experience is far more unique than those.'"*
>
> Bhakti Trilogy, 56

This devotee realizes that he has never experienced this bliss before and it cannot just be a concoction of the imagination. The devotee feels totally fulfilled. Even with the highest level of creativity, he could not imagine how the Lord would associate with him and what the nature of the experience would be. However, this devotee did have some previous glimpses or some shadow experiences. This shows that the experiences are not just "pie in the sky." It is not that we have to wait until our return to the spiritual world to experience and realize this highest level. Actually, when a devotee reaches perfection, Krishna takes him through all of these stages, introduces him to his original form, and introduces him to his position in the unfoldment of activities in Vrndavana. The devotee has had all of these experiences in the state of absorption, ecstasy, *bhava* and *prema*.

> *"In this way the devotee, assailed by doubts, falls to the ground, rolling in the dust. At times he reverts to constantly entreating the Lord to show Himself again. When the Lord does not appear he is grief-stricken and renews rolling on the ground so vigorously that he causes pain to his body. Finally, the devotee loses consciousness and goes into an ecstatic coma. Some time later he awakes, jumps up, sits down or weeps incessantly, wailing in a loud voice like a madman. Then suddenly the devotee stops all activities and retreats into a grave silence. On other occasions the afflicted devotee simply neglects all his regular religious and other duties, behaving whimsically and loosely. Again for no apparent reason he begins to speak incoherently like a lunatic. If a devotee friend approaches him with good intentions to pacify him and to make confidential enquiries about his condition, the devotee immediately reveals to his friend everything he has experienced. His friend tries to*

The Eighth Shower of Nectar

> *reason with him saying, 'My friend, your immense good fortune has enabled you to directly meet the Supreme Lord!'*
>
> *"For a while he becomes again calm and composed. Glowing with profound happiness he says, 'But alas! Shall I ever behold again His exquisite face?' In the next moment he is plunged into deep despondency and he cries out, 'How unfortunate I am! By the grace of a highly-enlightened and pure devotee of the Lord I was able to see the Lord's divine and beautiful form. But a mountain of misfortune obstructed me from performing even the slightest devotional service to the Lord. The sudden appearance of the Lord before me was certainly due to some incalculable heaps of piety, but because of immeasurably grievous offences He is now lost from my vision.'"*
>
> *Bhakti Trilogy, 56-57*

The devotee laments that, when the Lord appeared, he did not serve Him. Then he thinks that his grievous offenses from so many lifetimes have caused the Lord to disappear. The devotee's constant sense of humility and unworthiness is his qualification to receive. He has entirely surrendered and given everything; therefore, he is experiencing everything.

> "Or the bereft devotee thinks, 'Krishna is so merciful that He awarded me His direct audience although I am an insignificant speck floating in an ocean of bad qualities. This is because His mercy is causeless, hence He appeared to me. It is because of some unimaginable good fortune that the boundless ocean was for a few moments in the palm of my hand? But alas! My terrible faults have made this ocean disappear. My ignorance prevents me from discovering what actually happened. The whole experience has dumbfounded me and turned me into a fool. Where can I go? What shall I do? To whom shall I turn to for answers? I feel the world empty and void, absent of any companions, friends, or dear ones; a planet without a sanctuary; a world aflame in a raging forest fire eager to devour me. Under these circumstances, let me go to a secluded place away from crowds so I can meditate on this subject for some time.'
>
> "But even a quiet retreat does not

The Eighth Shower of Nectar

bring him tranquility. He calls out to the Lord, 'O my Supreme Master! My beautiful Lord! Your face is like the blossoming lotus. O reservoir of divine nectar, all of Vrndavana is intoxicated and aroused by the fragrance of Your transcendental body. The swaying garland of wildflowers around Your neck is attracting the honey-bees and making them restlessly buzz around it. How can I again have even a moment's glimpse of Your charming face? Only once have I relished the nectar of Your sublime beauty; will it be possible for me to again taste that delectable ambrosia? I humbly beg You to reveal Yourself to me.'

"In this way the devotee laments, sighing, and sometimes rolling in the dust. At times he collapses into an ecstatic state of unconsciousness or suddenly runs hither and thither like a madman. He sees Krishna in every direction and exuberantly laughs, sings and dances simultaneously. But in the very next moment he breaks down and cries hot tears of remorse. The devotee can thus pass the rest of his life in pursuit of such transcendental symptoms of ecstasy, but never more does he

> *pamper his body. In other words he is unconcerned about his physical well-being, feeling it unnecessary to enquire into its needs. After the demise of his body the devotee attains his eternal spiritual form (siddha-deha) and engages in the Lord's service. Factually, the devotee understands he has reached that siddha-deha stage when he becomes oblivious to his body. He thus thinks, 'The Supreme Lord, who is an ocean of compassion, has appeared on my plea, and He will personally engage me in His direct service and take me to His eternal abode.' With this understanding the devotee feels crowned with success."*
>
> Bhakti Trilogy, 57-58

So the devotee goes on with the rest of his existence in that physical body, acting somewhat as a mad person because he no longer has any taste for material existence. He no longer has any doubts about the illusions of material involvements. He completely feels overwhelmed when he thinks of how the Lord has been watching and providing through *guru*, the holy name, *sadhu-sanga* and *sastra*. It totally amazes him that all of his senses converge and receive reciprocation from the Lord. It entirely astounds him that the Lord is ready to give him everything but feels that nothing can sufficiently give enough glory and appreciation to the devotee; therefore, the Lord gives Himself fully. So the devotee spends the rest of his existence in and out of trance while waiting to put aside the physical garment. His identity is fully established and he is just waiting for the time when he will eternally experience that which the Lord has revealed. The Lord is gradually inviting him home.

Srila Visvanatha Cakravarti has given us a detailed analysis of the obstructions to our individual and collective devotional service. He has also given us such a sublime outline of the stages of progress up to prema. Now the challenge is before each of us to fully use what he has given us. How blessed we all are to be extended this opportunity through the blueprints given by such great *acaryas*, meant to facilitate us in returning to the realm of pure, enchanting, enduring and animated love.

Questions & Answers

Question: These experiences the devotee has while meeting Krishna reminded me of a pastime from *Krishna Book*. When the *gopis* heard Krishna's flute in the night, they left their activities to go meet Him in the Vrndavana forest. Those *gopis* who were restrained from leaving their homes left their bodies. For the first time I could see how they could leave their bodies in such a situation since a devotee in a physical body would pass out upon meeting the Lord.

Answer: Yes, it shows that their *laulya* or greed was so intense that they refused to miss associating with the Lord. If they could not associate in their physical bodies, then they went to join the association on the subtle plane.

We understand the power of hearing in the right environments because hearing stimulates the desire for experience and association. Krishna responds to every living entity's desires; therefore, the key lies in desiring the right thing with the right level of intensity. This only happens as a result of proper association. So as we share these topics, we have a chance to associate with Visvanatha Cakravarti Thakura. Furthermore, hearing these topics literally has a way of transforming consciousness. As we read *Madhurya-Kadambini*, we drop certain *karmic* patterns. Our devotion accelerates simply by hearing this sort of presentation. While we read, different devotees reflect on the material in different ways and undergo an internal cleansing. For this reason, *sadhu-sanga* or quality association is so important. It also helps us to see the areas that we need to work on. After discussing all of these high level topics, he again talks about the eighteen obstacles—envy, greed, fear, lamentations, etc. He lets us know what Krishna is offering so we can determine what we want. Do you want to hang onto all of this nonsense or do you want Krishna?

Question: Obviously the degree of surrender that is necessary to reach the highest stage of devotional

The Eighth Shower of Nectar

service is very difficult to achieve. In our movement, there are impurities and difficulties that seem to be surfacing to a particular degree at this time. So, to come to this level of surrender, there has to be trust and faith in authorities. Obviously the falldown of a *guru* could cause a great difficulty but at the same time, the individual must also have some responsibility to come to this level. The two would certainly be related; that is, the individual desire and also the position of the authority.

Answer: It is a deep reflection and question. I follow you fully. Yes, this is the whole science of *bhakti* wrapped up in your question. The living entity is an individualized expression of Krishna who has free will, and Krishna tunes into that. At the same time, we are products of different levels of socialization resulting from past lives and our present life. We are highly influenced by the quality of association that we have and the quality of connection or alignment. As we see in the schools, the student is distinctly influenced by the quality of the teacher. The parents, the teachers and the peers will all affect the students. One disadvantage of home schooling is that the child may miss out on the growth experienced in the association with other children unless they are very active within a home schooling community. All of these various aspects of education make up the character of the students. So if the *gurus* of an institution fall down or if the teachers of an academic institution leave their jobs or abuse the children, the experiences and levels of intense desire and greed in the individual for learning and growth will be affected. Why? Because these deviations will cause doubts if the environment is not sufficiently encouraging or if those who are catalysts for fanning the knowledge and love are not proper. However, Krishna will notice the individual. Unfortunately, the individual is often karmically connected to the environment and usually will remain locked into their surroundings.

Question: How can I protect myself but at the same time surrender?

Answer: Krishna, in the heart, knows the degree that we genuinely want to come to Him and at what pace. Therefore, we must always remember that it really depends on the living entity and Krishna, despite the external circumstances. Krishna arranges all kinds of fields of activities but ultimately, if the living entity is serious, Krishna will continue to bring them through. Even some of the most difficult experiences will act as catalysts to help that person. The most difficult obstacles that would seem to cause serious stagnation will have the opposite effect. They will simply intensify our desire for truth, love and association. These situations will always arise, but it has always been and always will be about Krishna and His parts and parcels. Krishna will be the one to arrange the necessary circumstances to bring us through based on our genuine desire to surrender. However, we all

The Eighth Shower of Nectar

have a duty to create an environment that makes it easier for ourselves and everyone else to accelerate. Ultimately, Krishna will respond in every single case according to the genuine desire and quality of surrender. In general we are more or less influenced by heredity and environment, for instance, a child may grow up with one or two parents or with a *karmi* or a devotee family. Nevertheless, Krishna is there and is responding to the quality of the individual regardless of what type of environment there is.

Question: Ultimately, if things go wrong in our devotional service, we really have no one to blame.

Answer: Yes, because we do not really fall down in one sense. Rather, our level of devotion gets exposed. We may pretend to have a certain level of devotion but as we continue, *maya* has a duty to reveal our real level. Based on this exposure, what will you do? In other words, the material body and the material world are places for deviation; therefore, when someone falls, it means that they have advanced to a certain level and have inwardly decided not to move any closer. So Krishna arranges to put them to the side in this way. However, whatever they have acquired will remain with them for the next round, later in this life or the next lifetime.

People are really not deviating although we use this word. Actually, individuals are just being categorized. Unfortunately a leader who does not reach the mark affects all of those under his or her authority because they are karmically and psychically locked up in the leader's consciousness. However, without trying to sound harsh, it is also arranged by Krishna due to all the different players such as *karma* and desires. Srila Visvanatha Cakravati has explained to us how scientific the influences of *karma* and desires are.

Question: So the sincere devotees will go on?

Answer: Yes, they will always go on despite the small setbacks. Setbacks will be processed in such a way that, when they are on track again, they will leap. Sometimes we explain how our advancement in spiritual life is usually not so vertical. It may be vertical from past lives but usually we come to work out certain issues and then we grow and work on more issues. Therefore, some of these experiences are necessary stagnations or tests for us to see our current capacity as we process and move on.

In an esoteric sense, when a person gets categorized, it is not necessarily a fall but it is really a clarification. Krishna is helping the person to see what they really have and do not have. Now the person can deal with all of these issues and try to work on what they lack in order to grow. Krishna gives us much more than our quality and then He gives us a chance to rise to that level. In other words, He may even seemingly give us a bit more than we can bear so that we can rely on Him more. He gives us a test so that we can rise to the next level. If we do not

The Eighth Shower of Nectar

come to that point, we get categorized at a certain level within that. However, the mercy is always greater than the law.

For instance, Srila Prabhupada has thousands of disciples around the world and, although some may be stagnant, they are still connected with Prabhupada. As they pass certain lessons and fail others, Srila Prabhupada has the responsibility to see that they receive additional help and support. All of the problems in the movement now such as falldowns, disturbances with the cows, or the lack of care for the children, the women, the elderly and the *brahmanas* are actually clarifying the realities. Now people can improve in these areas if they want. If they do not do their work, they will just get preoccupied in the revelation of the duality. Then the duality, anxieties, and pain become their *sadhana* instead of realizing the high gift before them and their chance to receive. Prabhupada has made so many wonderful arrangements and we need to rise to the level of that gift. This is the real question: How much will we come together as an international organization to recognize this wonderful gift? Srila Prabhupada reached down to pick us up from such low positions. Have we collectively and lovingly struggled to rise to that level or have we found ways to scapegoat without working on the real issues? Will people simply blame others or allow their pain to prevent them from catching up? This is happening now. Our movement as well as the world is currently in a state of processing, which means that some people will get sidetracked and others will gain more motivation to move towards these goals. For some people, these situations will make them detached from the duality because they will see its harshness.

We can use our difficulties to understand that we no longer want any part of such duality. On the other hand, the challenges can also cause us to feel victimized or inferior. Then the nourishment of the *sadhana* turns into *prajalpa* or anxiety, which then turns into anger, frustration and cynicism. For some people, their diet is now cynicism. Practically all of their writings or conversations involve cynicism. They constantly think, "That cannot work. Have you heard about this?" It becomes their whole *mantra*. They do not realize how much they are stagnating themselves. Then others think, "How do we avoid becoming embarrassments to Prabhupada? How do we reach out for each other? How do we learn from this situation so that it does not happen again?"

An amazing demarcation is happening in the movement. I see it when I travel. Devotees are either weakening or becoming very spiritually focused. However, in most cases, the distractions are overwhelming and people "lose it." Even some of those who strictly study the scriptures may simply study to beat someone else over the head with them. Then they can attack the different groups or show that *gurus* or institutions are useless. This turns into warfare, and warfare amongst *Vaisnavas* means *aparadhas*. At the end of the day, each person engaged in the *aparadhas* actually suffers, which

The Eighth Shower of Nectar

consequently stagnates Prabhupada's mission. It does not stop it but it hurts the general mission.

We can see that it was no accident when Krishna took away Srila Prabhupada, because we needed to undergo these experiences. For instance, when you are trying to wean a child off the breast or trying to help a child ride the bike without training wheels, you have to put them in a difficult situation and stand back in order to help them mature. When the child rode the bike with training wheels, he moved around fast and thought he was doing it all himself. When you remove the training wheels, they may fall down at first but gradually they start moving again. So there may be quite a few falldowns and some people may decide to simply put the bike away, thinking that it does not work anymore. Some people even blame the bike and claim it was never any good. Although the child may become angry or disturbed, such things have to happen for a child to really ride the bike himself. So this apparent confusion relates to maturation.

This is a very intense reflection that is applicable to our present situation. We must constantly do this. As we hear and reflect on the philosophy, we should also constantly make it relevant to our day-to-day experiences. Otherwise we will not be able to work on these issues in our society. This is another weakness that we have internationally. We have wonderful classes, Institute programs and VIHE seminars, but we have to carry these lessons with us in our daily activities and in our mind. Then when we deal with issues, we will understand how to use these spiritual technologies to make a difference.

Srila Visvanatha Cakravarti Thakura has so magnanimously come into this world from his residence in Goloka Vrndavana to warn us of the many obstacles on the royal path of devotion and most importantly to teach us very meticulously how to progress step by step in falling madly back in love with our worshipable Lord. We all have the choice of where we will repose our madness. We can remain mad for sense gratification or we can become fully transcendentally mad. Beloveds, let us invite the *kadambini* to shower *madhurya* on our external and internal environments, extinguishing the blazing forest fire of material attractions and attachments once and for all.

Glossary

Acarya: A spiritual master who teaches by his own example, and who sets the proper religious example for all human beings.

Adhibhautika: Misery caused by other living beings.

Adhidaivika: Misery or natural disturbances caused by the demigods.

Adhikara: The qualification or ability to understand spiritual matters due to previous spiritual activities.

Adhyatmika: Miseries arising from one's own body and mind.

Ahankara: False ego, by which the soul misidentifies with the material body.

Aisvarya: The Lord's majestic, opulent aspect.

Akincana-Krishna: The Lord, who is dear to those who are without material possessions.

Anartha-nivrtti: A stage in the progressive development of devotion to Lord Krishna in which one is freed from unwanted desires and karmic reactions; cleansing the heart of all unwanted things.

Anarthas: Unwanted material desires in the heart that pollute one's consciousness, such as pride, hate, envy, lust, greed, anger and desires for distinction, adoration, wealth, etc.

Anisthita-bhajana-kriya: The stage where devotional practices are firmly established.

Aparadha: An offense.

Aparadhottha: *Anarthas* coming from offenses.

Aprarabdha: Sinful reactions not yet manifest.

Apratipatti: Being incapable of performing devotional service even though one is unhampered by *laya* and *visepa*.

Arati: A traditional Vedic ceremony during which offerings of incense, ghee lamp, flower, etc. are offered to the Deity of the Lord.

Arcana: The procedures followed for worshiping the *arca-vigraha*, the Deity in the temple; engaging all the senses in the service of the Lord.

Asakti: Attachment.

Asramas: The four spiritual orders according to the Vedic social system: *brahmacarya* (student life), *grhastha* (householder life), *vanaprastha* (retirement) and *sannyasa* (renunciation).

Atyantiki: Completely.

Avant-garde: An intelligentsia that develops new or experimental concepts especially in the arts.

Babaji: A person who dwells alone in one place and leads a life of meditation, penance and austerity; renounced order beyond *sannyasa*, in which one chants and reads.

Bahu-desavarttini: A line of argument in logic stating the similarities, which are in many areas but not in all areas, between two different subjects.

Glossary

Bhajana: Intimate devotional service; chanting devotional songs in a small group, usually accompanied by musical instruments; solitary chanting.

Bhajana-kriya: The third phase of *sraddha* where devotional activities are executed under the instruction of the *guru*.

Bhajana-kutira: A small hut or cottage where a Vaisnava or saintly person performs his *bhajana* or personal meditation.

Bhajananandi: A devotee who performs his devotional activities in seclusion, not attempting to preach; a devotee who is satisfied to cultivate devotional service for himself.

Bhakta: A devotee of the Lord; one who performs devotional service (*bhakti*).

Bhakta-vatsalya: The Lord, who is affectionate to His devotees

Bhakti: Devotional service to the Supreme Lord.

Bhakti-lata: The creeper of devotion.

Bhaktyuttha: That which stems from *bhakti*.

Bhava: The stage of transcendental love experienced after transcendental affection; manifestation of ecstatic symptoms in the body of a devotee.

Bhava-bhakti: Rendering spontaneous service, which is superior to regulative devotional service.

Bhoga: Material sense enjoyment; or, food before it has been offered to the Deity.

Bijam: Seed.

Brahmacari: A celibate student under the care of a spiritual master.

Brahmana: A member of the most intelligent class, according to the four Vedic occupational divisions of society.

Camara: A yak-tail fan used in Deity worship.

Darsana: The act of seeing or being seen by the Deity in the temple or by a spiritually advanced person.

Deva: A demigod or a saintly person.

Dhama: A holy place.

Dhama-aparadha: An offense against the holy places.

Dharma: Religious principles; one's natural occupation.

Duskrtottha: Stemming from sinful activity.

Ekadesavarttini: A line of argument in logic stating the only similarity existing between two different subjects.

Gandharva: Celestial denizens of heavenly planets who possess mystical powers as well as an innate capability to sing.

Gopis: The cowherd girls of Vraja, who are generally the counterparts of Sri Krishna's *hladini-sakti*, Srimati Radharani.

Gosthy-anandis: A Vaisnava who is interested in spreading Krishna consciousness.

Gosvami: A person who has his senses under full control; the title of a person in the renounced order of life, *sannyasa*.

Guru: Spiritual master.

Guru-aparadha: An offense against the spiritual master.

Glossary

Gurukula: A school of Vedic learning. Boys begin at five years old and live as celibate students, guided by a spiritual master.

Isvara: A controller. Krishna is *paramesvara*, the supreme controller.

Jati: Caste or creed.

Jiva: The eternal individual soul.

Jnana: Transcendental knowledge.

Kadambini: A long line or bank of clouds.

Kali-yuga: The age of quarrel and hypocrisy, which began five thousand years ago and lasts a total of 432,000 years.

Kama: Lust.

Karma: Material activities, for which one incurs subsequent reactions.

Karma-kanda: The division of the Vedas which deals with fruitive activities performed for the purpose of gradual purification of the grossly entangled materialist.

Karmi: One engaged in *karma* (fruitive activity); a materialist.

Kasaya: Adulteration in the consciousness: to maintain lust, greed, pride, anger, and so on while chanting the holy name.

Kirtana: Chanting of the Lord's holy names.

Klesaghni: Description of devotional service indicating that it reduces or nullifies all kinds of suffering.

Laya: Attacks of sleeping bouts during hearing, chanting, and remembering.

Lila: A transcendental "pastime" or activity performed by God or His devotee.

Lobha: Greed.

Madhurya: Spiritual sweetness.

Madhvacarya: A great thirteenth century Vaisnava spiritual master, who preached the theistic philosophy of pure dualism.

Madhyama-adhikari: The second or intermediate level of the three types of devotees.

Manjaris: The young female assistants of the *sakhis* or girlfriends of Srimati Radharani, all between the ages of 6-9 years.

Mataji: Mother.

Maya: The external energy of the Supreme Lord, which covers the conditioned soul and does not allow him to understand the Supreme Personality of Godhead.

Mayavadis: Any person who thinks that the name and form of the Supreme Lord are made of *maya*, or material energy; ultimately, *mayavadis* want to merge into the impersonal *brahman* (*sayujya-mukti*), thereby committing spiritual suicide.

Misra-bhakti: Where devotion is not purely spiritual but mixed with material desires.

Moksa: Liberation from material bondage.

Mrdanga: A two-headed clay drum used for *kirtana* performances and congregational chanting.

Nama-aparadha: An offense against the holy name of the Lord.

Nistha: Unflinching faith, steadfast devotion; the stage after *anartha-nivrtti*.

Niyamaksama: A part of *bhajana-kriya* where vows to follow certain rules are made repeatedly but are not kept.

Pandita: A learned Vedic scholar whose knowledge is based on scripture.

Parampara: The disciplic succession system of spiritual knowledge beginning with the Lord Himself, and continuing down to the present day.

Prajalpa: Idle talk on mundane subjects.

Pramana: That which establishes the authenticity of a subject.

Prarabdha: Reactions of past activities that have already begun to fructify, offering both sinful reactions as well as pious results.

Pratistha: Fame.

Prema: Love; pure and unbreakable love of God; the stage after *bhava* (*rati*), where the soul has attained both self-realization and God realization.

Preyasi: Most beloved wife or consort.

Puja: Worship, usually in the form of making offerings to the Deity of the Lord.

Pujari: A priest, specifically one engaged in temple Deity worship.

Purna: Complete, whole.

Raga-bhakti: The spontaneous devotional process marked by an intense desire to achieve *prema*, and where the following of scriptural edicts becomes a secondary consideration.

Raksasa: A class of *asura* or ungodly people. The Raksasa are always opposed to God's will. Generally, they are man-eaters and have grotesque forms.

Rasa: The transcendental "taste" of a particular spiritual relationship with the Supreme Lord.

Rati: The ripened stage of loving attachments, or *prema-nistha*.

Rtvik: A surrogate priest who performs Vedic ceremonies in the absence of another.

Ruci: Liking, taste; the stage after *nistha*, when a strong taste for devotional service arises in the devotee.

Sadhaka: One who practices regulated devotional service.

Sadhana-bhakti: There are nine limbs to the practice of *sadhana-bhakti*: hearing, chanting, remembering, worshiping, praying, rendering service, carrying out the orders of the Lord, being a friend of the Lord and completely surrendering to the Lord.

Sadhu: Saintly person.

Sadhu-sanga: Association with *sadhus*.

Sahajiya: A class of so-called devotees who, considering God cheap, ignore the scriptural injunctions and try to imitate the Lord's pastimes.

Sakti: Spiritual energy.

Samsara: The cycle of repeated birth and death in the material world.

Sanatana: Eternal, having no beginning or end.

Sankirtana: The congregational chanting of the holy name, fame, and pastimes of the Lord; preaching.

Sannyasa: The renounced order of life for spiritual culture.

Sannyasi: A person in the renounced order.

Sastra: Revealed scripture; Vedic literature.

Seva-aparadha: Offenses in devotional service.

Glossary

Siddha-deha: The pure spiritual form of the devotee engaged in pure devotional service. The spiritual identity of the devotee revealed to him by his *maha-bhagavat* spiritual master.

Sraddha: Firm faith and confidence.

Suddha-bhakta: A pure devotee.

Suddha-bhakti: Pure, unconditional, unmotivated devotional service.

Sukrti: Results accrued from pious activity.

Svarupa: The living entity's original eternal relationship of service to the Lord, the real form of the soul.

Taranga-rangini: A stage in *bhajana-kriya* where the devotee becomes attached to material wealth, adoration, and distinction.

Utsahamayi: That which is saturated with steady determination and perseverance.

Vaidhi-bhakti: Regulative devotional service devoid of *lobha* and prompted by scriptural injunctions.

Vaisnava: A devotee of Lord Visnu.

Vaisya: A member of the mercantile and agricultural class, according to the four Vedic occupational divisions of society.

Vastu: The supreme shelter and source of all potencies (*cit*, *maya*, and *jiva*).

Vatsalya: The relationship with Krishna as His parent.

Vedanta-sutra: The philosophical treatise written by Vyasadeva, consisting of succinct aphorisms that embody the essential meaning of the *Upanisads*.

Vijnana: The practical realization of spiritual knowledge.

Viksepa: The tendency to talk of material things during chanting; one of the five detriments that hinder the devotee from attaining unflinching determination or *nisthita bhakti*.

Visaya-sangara: One of the six stages of *bhajana-kriya* where the devotee is caught in a conflict with his material attachments between his desire to sever his attachments and the desire to enjoy them.

Yajna: Sacrifice.

Yoga: Spiritual discipline to link oneself with the Supreme.

Yuga: An "age." There are four *yugas*, which cycle perpetually: Satya-yuga, Treta-yuga, Dvapara-yuga and Kali-yuga. As the ages proceed from Satya to Kali, religion and the good qualities of men gradually decline.

Bibliography

Atwater, P.M.H. *Children of the New Millennium*. New York: Three Rivers Press, 1999.

Thakura, Visvanatha Cakravarti. *The Bhakti Trilogy: Delineations on the Esoterics of Pure Devotion*. Translated by Sarvabhavana Dasa. Edited by Krsna-rupa Devi Dasi. Calcutta, India: Harmonist Publications, n.d.

Index

Abhay Charan, 41
abhyasa, 131
abuse, 17, 18, 25, 77, 82, 88, 95, 189
acarya, 14, 30, 38, 39, 44, 45, 48, 89, 107, 142, 143, 144, 145, 187
adhibhautika, 164
adhidaivika, 164
adhikara, 111
adhyatmika, 164
aham mameti, 68, 175
ahankara, 58
aisvarya, 49
Akincana-Krishna, 107
Alachua, 27
America, 25, 63
anartha-nivrtti, 81, 83
anarthas, 10, 22, 67, 81, 83, 85, 90, 91, 92, 93, 97, 98, 103, 104, 106, 109, 110, 112, 115, 127, 173
anisthita, 71, 75, 126, 127
anisthita-bhakti, 126
anugraha, 107, 172
anxiety, 16, 57, 59, 78, 84, 87, 100, 118, 155, 163, 174, 193, 194
aparadha, 11, 67, 99, 100, 104, 127, 129, 194
aparadhottha, 81, 92
aprarabdha, 65, 85
apratipatti, 117
arati, 136
arcana, 143
Arjuna, 107
asa-bandha, 44

asakti, 139, 141, 142
asramas, 19, 27
assassination, 3
atheists, 88, 151
atma-nivedana, 143
atyantiki, 104
Audarya, 170
Aurangzeb, Samrat, 1
austerities, 36, 46
Austria, 2, 62
autocracy, 25, 37
Avant-garde, 83
babaji, 154
Back to Godhead, 58
Bahaullah, 3
bahu-desavarttini, 104
Baladeva, 4, 5, 6, 7, 14, 21
Balarama, 93
balotpadika, 70
benediction, 60, 107, 166
Bhagavad-gita, 7, 30, 43, 47, 107
Bhagavatam, 4, 10, 39, 137
bhajana, 6, 70, 71, 104, 105, 115, 129, 133, 134, 141, 142, 143, 148, 149
bhajana-kriya, 70, 71
bhajana-kutira, 6
bhajananandis, 156
bhajanas, 36
bhakta, 33, 45, 70, 94, 137, 138, 169
bhakta-vatsalya, 33, 45
bhakti, 12, 13, 22, 25, 30, 31, 32, 33, 35, 36, 40, 41, 42, 43, 44, 51, 54,

55, 56, 57, 59, 62, 70, 75, 76, 78, 81, 88, 89, 91, 105, 121, 122, 125, 128, 131, 138, 139, 143, 148, 152, 153, 158, 189
bhakti-lata-bija, 105
bhakti-nistha, 125
Bhaktisiddhanta, 2, 3, 8
Bhaktivinoda, 1
bhaktyuttha, 81, 97
Bhatta, Raghunatha, 142
bhava, 29, 53, 139, 141, 142, 147, 148, 149, 151, 152, 162, 182
bhava-bhakti, 149
bhoga, 72, 77
bhoga-tyaga, 72
bija, 65
blame, 50, 93, 111, 191, 193, 195
blasphemy, 101, 158
Brahma, 176
brahmacari, 12, 13, 27, 101
brahmana, 5, 11, 18, 94, 193
brahminical, 62, 63
Brghu, 84
Buddha, 158
businessmen, 78, 91
Caitanya-caritamrta, 30, 43
Cakravarti, Visvanatha, 1, 3, 4, 5, 6, 7, 8, 9, 11, 12, 14, 19, 29, 31, 40, 46, 55, 57, 60, 61, 65, 79, 90, 94, 97, 98, 102, 111, 115, 121, 122, 131, 134, 142, 161, 163, 165, 177, 187, 188, 196
camara, 98
Christians, 87
communication, 26
community, 1, 3, 26, 27, 97
compassion, 37, 60, 65, 67, 68, 90, 101, 119, 124, 168, 172, 173, 180, 186
cooking, 118
cult, 2
cynicism, 194
Damodara, 4, 5

darsana, 9, 93, 106
dasya, 143, 169, 173
dasya-bhakta, 173
deceit, 173
degradation, 71
Deities, 1, 2, 12, 13, 14, 15, 30, 38, 42, 46, 74, 98, 118, 119, 137
demigods, 42, 127, 158, 159, 162, 176
demons, 1, 2, 38, 78
dependence, 117, 173
depression, 27, 59, 61, 94
devas, 158, 164
dhama, holy, 18, 92, 93, 94
dhama-aparadha, 92
dharma, 31, 156
disciple, 70
disqualifications, overcoming, 173
duskrtottha, 81, 83
ekadesavarttini, 103
enviousness, 34, 61, 164
ethics, 3, 125
faith, 3, 49, 53, 54, 57, 58, 69, 70, 73, 89, 105, 117, 121, 122, 125, 189
faithlessness, 61
fanaticism, 122
feminism, 18
France, 2, 62
fundamentalists, 17
gandharva, 162
gardening, 91
Gaudiya Vaisnava, 4, 6, 7
Gaudiya Vaisnava siddhanta, 7
Gaudiyas, 7
Gauranga, 136
ghana-tarala, 72
Goloka, 196
gopi, 180, 187
gosthy-anandis, 156
Gosvamis, 9, 129
Govardhana, 8, 14, 38
Govardhana-sila, 14

Govinda, 7
guna, 143
Gundica Temple, 66, 97
guru, 8, 10, 20, 39, 40, 42, 48, 49, 96, 101, 138, 154, 155, 186, 189, 194
guru-aparadha, 101
gurukula, 18
Hardwar, 93
Hari, 115
hatha-yoga, 49
Hiranyakasipu, 78
Hridayananda Goswami, 129
Hrsikesa, 93
impersonalism, 48
impersonalists, 2, 79
India, 63
intoxication, 22, 61, 92, 161, 164
ISKCON, 78
Isvara, 37
isvaras, 91
Jaipur, 2, 6
Janmastami, 28
jati, 152
Jerusalem, 93
Jesus, 3, 142, 158
jiva, 1, 6, 7, 31, 41, 102, 103, 142
jnana, 4, 12, 40, 46, 55, 56, 103, 139
jnana-misra-bhakti, 55
kadambini, 29, 196
kala, 79
Kali-yuga, 2, 15
kama, 13, 139
kama-gayatri, 13
karma, 19, 20, 40, 42, 48, 49, 55, 56, 79, 80, 85, 86, 87, 88, 92, 95, 106, 107, 111, 113, 192
karma-kanda, 42, 48, 113
karma-misra-bhakti, 55
karmi, 191
karmic, 23, 24, 50, 78, 79, 85, 87, 88, 95, 111, 120, 188
karmically, 120, 190, 192

kasaya, 118
Katyayani-vrata, 157
Kaviraja, 9, 10, 11, 12, 13, 14, 20, 22
kayiki, 121, 122
kirtana, 36, 116, 133, 134, 143, 154
klesaghni, 56
Krishna Book, 187
Krishna-aparadha, 101
Krishnadasa, 13, 14, 79
kriya-yoga, 49
kuta, 65
laulya, 56, 150, 166, 188
laya, 115, 117
leprosy, 10, 11
lila, 143, 157, 158
lobha, 97, 109
Madhavendra Puri, 150
madhurya, 4, 29, 47, 169, 170, 173, 196
madhurya-bhakta, 173
Madhurya-Kadambini, 29, 81, 161, 188
madhurya-rasa, 4, 170
Madhvacarya, 4, 5, 6, 7, 142
Madhvacaryas, 4
Madhvacarya-sampradaya, 4, 5, 6
madhyama-adhikari, 34, 35
Mahabharata, 30
Mahaprabhu, 4, 6, 9, 11, 156
manasiki, 121, 122
manjaris, 158
Manu-samhita, 17
mataji, 101
maya, 2, 19, 20, 58, 61, 62, 66, 67, 89, 95, 105, 107, 191
mayavadis, 2
Mecca, 93
misra, 54, 55, 59, 61, 65, 72
misra-bhakti, 55, 61, 65, 72
moksa, 156
Mormons, 3
mrdanga, 133

Muhammad, 3, 142
Mukunda, 3, 14, 142
Muslim, 3
nama aparadha, 92, 99, 100
Narayana, 6, 7
Nectar of Devotion, 30, 153
neophytes, 30, 47, 72, 128, 139, 158
Nigeria, 158
nistha, 104, 139
nisthita, 71, 115, 126, 127
nisthita-bhakti, 115, 126, 127
nivrtti, 81
niyamaksama, 74, 75
opulence, 92, 103, 108, 169, 172, 176, 177
overeating, 116
pada-sevana, 143
pandita, 5, 9, 12, 13, 55
parampara, 144
Pariksit Maharaja, 21
phobia, 82
Prabhupada Lilamrta, 41
Prahlada, 78
prajalpa, 62, 64, 194
pramana, 153
prarabdha, 65, 85
pratistha, 11, 97, 109
prayiki, 104
prema, 20, 29, 70, 104, 105, 136, 139, 141, 150, 151, 158, 161, 162, 163, 164, 165, 166, 171, 182, 187
pretenders, 138, 139
preyasi, 179
principles, 69, 105
psychologists, 82
puja, 91, 97, 109, 158
pujari, 118
pujas, 42
purna, 104
Radha-Damodara Vilasa, 157
Radharani, 4, 5, 6, 7, 14, 21, 111, 157, 158, 166, 180

raga-bhakti, 56
raga-bhakti-uttha, 152
Raghunatha dasa Goswami, 13, 142
raksasa, 137, 162
Ramanujacarya, 142
Ram ayana, 137
rasa, 30, 42, 47, 172, 180
rasasvada, 120
rati, 104
religion, 11, 43, 51, 53, 125
religionists, 3
repentance, 22
Romans, 64
rtvik, 19, 27
ruci, 70, 131, 132, 133, 134, 139, 141, 145, 148
sadhaka, 152
sadhana, 56, 69, 103, 104, 128, 193, 194
sadhana-bhakti, 56, 69, 103, 128
sadhu, 10, 11, 42, 46, 101, 102, 105, 109, 112, 123, 138, 142, 154, 155, 186, 188
sadhu-sanga, 46, 105, 186, 188
sahajiyas, 1, 2, 10
sakhya, 42, 43, 143, 169
saksat bhakti-visayini, 121
saksat-bhakti, 122
sakti, 31
Samrat Aurangzeb, 1
samsara, 164
sanatana, 142
sankirtana, 3
sannyasis, 8, 23, 27, 95
Sanskrit, 9, 11
Sarasvati, 2
sastra, 10, 48, 138, 155, 157, 186
sectarianism, 17
servitorship, 102, 169
seva-aparadha, 98, 118
siddha-deha, 186
siddhanta, 7, 14, 16

siddhic, 55
sila, 13
smarana, 116
socialization, 24, 25, 157, 189
Socrates, 3
Spiritual Warriors, 38
sraddha, 53, 54, 61, 70
sravana, 116, 143
Srimad-Bhagavatam, 7, 8, 18, 29, 31, 32, 33, 36, 40, 43, 68, 106, 120
subhada, 56
Sudarsana, 177
suddha-bhakti, 13, 30, 56, 72, 139
Sukadeva Goswami, 21
sukrti, 61
sukrtottha, 91
svabhaviki, 70
svarupa, 47, 110
Switzerland, 62
Syamasundara, 150
synagogues, 117
tambora, 133
taranga-rangini, 75
teachers, 18, 189
teamship, 9
technologies, spiritual, 196
tirthas, 93
transcendence, 58, 63, 130
truthfulness, 3, 68
Upendra, 122
utsahamayi, 71
uttama-adhikari, 151
vaciki, 121, 122
vaidha-bhakti-uttha, 152
Vaisnava acaryas, 43
Vaisnava siddhanta, 5, 41, 49
Vaisnavism, 2, 4
vaisya, 11
Vaiyasaki, 157
vandana, 143
vastu, 132

vatsalya, 42, 169, 173
vatsalya-bhakta, 173
vatsalya-rasa, 42
Vedanta-sutra, 7
Vedas, 36, 136
Vidyabhusana, Baladeva, 4, 5, 6, 7, 14, 21
VIHE, 94, 195
vijnana, 4, 139
viksepa, 116, 117
visaya-sangara, 73
Visnu, 84
vows, 74
vrata, 36, 157
vyudha-vikalpa, 72
yadrcchaya, 32
yajnas, 36
Yamuna, 93
yoga, 36, 40, 55, 56
yoga-misra-bhakti, 55
yugas, 107
Zoroaster, 3

About The Author

Bhakti-Tirtha Swami Krishnapada was born John E. Favors in a pious, God-fearing family. As a child evangelist he appeared regularly on television. As a young man he was a leader in Dr. Martin Luther King, Jr.'s civil rights movement. At Princeton University he became president of the student council and also served as chairman of the Third World Coalition. Although his main degree is in psychology, he has received accolades in many other fields, including politics, African studies, Indology and international law.

Bhakti-Tirtha Swami,s books are used as reference texts in universities and leadership organizations throughout the world. Many of his books have been printed in English, German, French, Spanish, Portuguese, Macedonian, Croatian, Russian, Hebrew, Slovenian, Balinese and Italian.

His Holiness has served as Assistant Coordinator for penal reform programs in the State of New Jersey, Office of the Public Defender, and as a director of several drug abuse clinics in the United States. In addition, he has been a special consultant for Educational Testing Services in the U.S.A. and has managed campaigns for politicians. Bhakti-Tirtha Swami gained international recognition as a representative of the Bhaktivedanta Book Trust, particularly for his outstanding work with scholars in the former communist countries of Eastern Europe.

Bhakti-Tirtha Swami directly oversees projects in the United States (particularly Washington D.C., Potomac, Maryland, Detroit, Pennsylvania, West Virginia), West Africa, South Africa, Switzerland, France, Croatia and Bosnia. He also serves as the director of the American Federation of Vaisnava Colleges and Schools.

In the United States, Bhakti-Tirtha Swami is the founder and director of the Institute for Applied Spiritual Technology, director of the International Committee for Urban Spiritual Development and one of the international coordinators of the Seventh Pan African Congress. Reflecting his wide range of interests, he is also a member of the Institute for Noetic Sciences, the Center for Defense Information, the United Nations Association for America, the National Peace Institute Foundation, the World Future Society and the Global Forum of Spiritual and Parliamentary Leaders.

Author's Bio

A specialist in international relations and conflict resolution, Bhakti-Tirtha Swami constantly travels around the world and has become a spiritual consultant to many high-ranking members of the United Nations, to various celebrities and to several chiefs, kings and high court justices. In 1990 His Holiness was coronated as a high chief in Warri, Nigeria in recognition of his outstanding work in Africa and the world. In recent years, he has met several times with then-President Nelson Mandela of South Africa to share visions and strategies for world peace.

In addition to encouraging self-sufficiency through the development of schools, clinics, farm projects and cottage industries, Bhakti-Tirtha Swami conducts seminars and workshops on principle centered leadership, spiritual development, interpersonal relationships, stress and time management and other pertinent topics. He is also widely acknowledged as a viable participant in the resolution of global conflict.

Leadership for an Age of Higher Consciousness I
Administration from a Metaphysical Perspective

by B.T. Swami
(Swami Krishnapada)

$23.00 hardbound ISBN #1-885414-02-1
$14.95 softbound ISBN #1-885414-05-6
320 pages, 2nd edition

"An example in the truest sense of global principle-centered leadership, Swami Krishnapada manages to take consciousness-raising to its highest platform of self-realized actuality in humanizing the workplace. My experience in working with all of the nations of the world convinces me that such a book is the corporate leadership guide for the coming millennium."

> The Honorable Pierre Adossama
> Director, Labor Relations (Retired)
> International Labor Organization
> United Nations

The Leader In You

Leadership in any capacity has taken on such awesome proportions that even the best leaders must find innovative and creative ways to deal with today's complex situations. *Leadership for an Age of Higher Consciousness: Administration from a Metaphysical Perspective* is a ground breaking self-help manual written for those who seek to develop a more penetrating perspective and greater effectiveness in the leadership process. This book is relevant for heads of government, organizations and families, and for anyone seeking greater insight into self-leadership.

Order on the web at **www.ifast.net**

Leadership for an Age of Higher Consciousness II
Ancient Wisdom For Modern Times

Become An Authentic Leader

by B.T. Swami
(Swami Krishnapada)

$23.00 hardbound ISBN #1-885414-11-0
$14.95 softbound ISBN #1-885414-12-9
209 pages, 1st edition

"Good leadership is not just a matter of making things happen; it is a matter of making essential things happen, making important and productive things happen, and helping people feel good about what is happening. Leaders need to have a vision, but they also need to know how to convince others that their vision can manifest, and how to empower them to participate in the mission of bringing the vision about."

—*Excerpt from Leadership for an Age of Higher Consciousness, Vol. 2*

In this sequel to his internationally acclaimed *Leadership for an Age of Higher Consciousness: Administration from a Metaphysical Perspective*, His Holiness Bhakti-Tirtha Swami Krishnapada explores the greatness of two famous leaders from the Vedic tradition of ancient India. Addressing the leader within each of us, B.T. Swami shows us that the greatest leaders see themselves as servants first, they place integrity and character before personal gain, and they know how to tap into the help that is available from both the earthly and spiritual realms. True servant leaders are animated visionaries who cultivate divine power to transform diverse individuals with scattered goals into communities with a unified, sacred mission.

Order on the web at **www.ifast.net**

Spiritual Warrior I

Uncovering Spiritual Truths in Psychic Phenomena

by B.T. Swami
(Swami Krishnapada)

$12.95 softbound   ISBN #1-885414-01-3
200 pages, 2nd edition

"As we rapidly approach the new millennium, more and more people are searching for spiritual answers to the meaning and purpose of life. The search, of course, begins with Self, and Swami Krishnapada's book, *Spiritual Warrior*, provides a practical companion for the journey of the initiate. I am honored to recommend it."

> Gordon-Michael Scallion
> Futurist; Editor,
> *Earth Changes Report*
> Matrix Institute, Inc.

Ancient Mysteries Revealed!

Get ready for a roller-coaster ride into the intriguing realm of ancient mysteries! It is rare to find the subjects in this book handled in such a piercing and straightforward way. *Spiritual Warrior: Uncovering Spiritual Truths in Psychic Phenomena* focuses on the spiritual essence of many topics that have bewildered scholars and scientists for generations, such as extraterrestrials, the pyramids and psychic intrusion. A fresh perspective is revealed, inviting the reader to expand the boundaries of the mind and experience a true and lasting connection with the inner self.

Order on the web at **www.ifast.net**

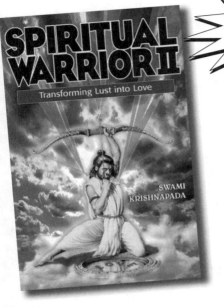

Also available on:
9 CD set $60 or
10 Audio tape set $45

Spiritual Warrior II

Transforming Lust into Love

by B.T. Swami
(Swami Krishnapada)

$20.00 hardbound ISBN #1-885414-03-x
$12.95 softbound ISBN #1-885414-09-9
248 pages

"Spiritual Warrior II: Transforming Lust into Love is a book to savor and treasure, a book that needs to be read and reread because of its spiritual potency and priceless value for everyday living....I am currently on my second and even third reading of certain chapters of this divinely inspired offering.... Everyone needs a copy of this book."

—Terry Cole-Whittaker. D.D.
Author of *What You Think of Me Is None of My Business*

Opening Your Heart

Today's world is suffering from an overdose of lust, while people everywhere are starving for love. In *Spiritual Warrior II*, Bhakti-Tirtha Swami offers profound insight into the critical issues of the body, mind, and spirit that touch us all. Tough questions are addressed, such as: What is love? Where does lust come from? How can sexuality become a constructive force? How can we have better relationships? Provided with insightful answers stemming from a broad, compassionate perspective deeply grounded in spirituality, we are shown how to live from the heart, loving ourselves, one another and God.

Order on the web at **www.ifast.net**

Spiritual Warrior III

Solace for the Heart in Difficult Times

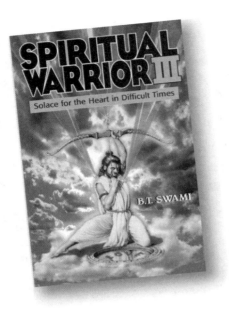

by B.T. Swami
(Swami Krishnapada)

$23.00 hardbound ISBN #1-885414-06-4
$14.95 softbound ISBN #1-885414-07-2
324 pages

Start reconstructing a loving society around you!

Has your day-to-day struggle become minute-by-minute? How do we cope with life in these trying times? And what can we do to ease the pain of a suffering society? These genuine issues, and many more, are addressed in *"Spiritual Warrior III: Solace for the Heart In Difficult Times."* Bhakti-Tirtha Swami, a devout spiritual warrior himself, provides critical insight into the powerful position of spiritual warriors in this new millennium. This imperative survival guide gives techniques and an in-depth philosophical understanding necessary to purposely help yourself and others throughout times of crisis.

"Fear and love do not go together. Fear is constricting, self-centered and self-conscious, whereas love is expansive, selfless and directed toward service. To become effective spiritual warriors, we must learn to cultivate genuine love, courage, and compassion and come to depend on our inner faculties rather than externals. This allows us to understand our own true nature more deeply, and to behave more like the children and servants of God that we are. Then, firmly established in a higher state of consciousness, we can serve others—and the world—from the deepest, most aware and loving aspect of ourselves during these challenging times."

—*excerpt from Spiritual Warrior III*

Order on the web at **www.ifast.net**

Also available on audio cassette!

The Beggar I

Meditations and Prayers on the Supreme Lord

by B.T. Swami
(Swami Krishnapada)

$11.95 softbound
160 pages, ISBN #1-885414-00-5

Serenity in the Lord

Deeply penetrating reflections in the form of a personal dialogue with God remind the reader of the necessity to dedicate time to spiritual growth along with secular pursuits. Written in an easily readable, non-sectarian style, this book explores such topics as patience, tolerance, humility, compassion and determination. The author presents these subjects not as quaint meusings from another age but as necessary tools for maintaining sanity in a far-from-normal world full of conflict and stress.

"Now, my dear Lord, I am completely confused. I have tried to attract You, but I see I have nothing to attract You with. I am a pretender. I want Your kingdom, without You. I am a criminal who has tried to plead innocent, and now I have nowhere to hide, no presentations to make. What am I to do, dear Lord?

"Then I heard the Lord say: 'You have always been, and always will be, dear to Me, but you do not believe it. Therefore, you separate us by being an enemy to yourself. Come on, My child, and experience what it is to be fully dear to Me.'"

Excerpt from *The Beggar*

Order on the web at **www.ifast.net**

The Beggar II

Crying Out for the Mercy

Commune with the Lord

by B.T. Swami
(Swami Krishnapada)

$11.95 softbound ISBN #1-885414-04-8
184 pages

This deeply inspirational offering to the Lord and His devotees is Bhakti-Tirtha Swami's wonderful follow-up book to *The Beggar I: Meditations and Prayers on the Supreme Lord*. You'll love this all new collection of prayers, meditations and essays, as they make you cry, laugh, and most of all, commune with that innermost part of you that's crying out for the mercy. This book is a must read, so order yours now, and get ready for the Lord's mercy!

"Immediately I felt the weight of my deficiencies, and realized how polluted my consciousness had become. The voice continued speaking, giving me a welcome distraction.
'Despite your many deficiencies, I have been drawn to you by the intensity of your greed and desperation for transcendence. In fact, I have been sanctioned by higher authority to reveal your shortcomings to you. I therefore beg you to listen closely, for this is a rare opportunity that may not come again for many lifetimes.'
I braced myself for a rude awakening..." —*excerpts from The Beggar II*

Order on the web at **www.ifast.net**

The Beggar III

False Ego: The Greatest Enemy of the Spiritual Leader

Release Your True Self

by B.T. Swami
(Swami Krishnapada)

$12.95 softbound ISBN #1-885414-10-2
215 pages

"Bhakti-Tirtha Swami's books are all written to facilitate us in keeping our highest Self in charge of our lives as we move toward our greatest potential and highest good. The Beggar III is his latest contribution to helping us do the often-difficult inner work of understanding that our life force is our God force. Typical of all true leaders, he teaches by loving, living example."

John T. Chissell, M.D.
Author: *Pyramids of Power*

"...Selflessness is the ingredient most lacking in today's world, because people misunderstand the purpose and principle behind this wonderful science. Genuine selflessness is not thinking less of yourself, but thinking of yourself less.

"My mentor continued: 'Selflessness doesn't mean to give up pursuing adventurous goals, but rather to attach ourselves to transcendental goals. Actual selflessness means we must genuinely access humility and submissiveness. This can be very scary, because we normally identify humility and submissiveness with low self-esteem.'"

—*excerpts from The Beggar III*

Order on the web at **www.ifast.net**

Reflections on Sacred Teachings

Volume One: Sri Siksastaka

Explore Timeless Wisdom

by B.T. Swami
(Swami Krishnapada)

$14.95, softbound ISBN #1-885414-13-7
260 pages

"O Govinda! Feeling Your separation, I am considering a moment to be like twelve years or more. Tears are flowing from my eyes like torrents of rain and I am feeling all vacant in the world in Your absence."

"Lord Caitanya Mahaprabhu instructed His disciples to write books on the science of Krishna, a task which those who follow Him have continued to carry out down to the present day. The elaborations and expositions on the philosophy taught by Lord Caitanya are in fact most voluminous, exacting and consistent due to the system of disciplic succession. Although Lord Caitanya was widely renowned as a scholar in His youth, He left only eight verses, called *Siksastaka*. These eight verses clearly reveal His mission and precepts."

– A.C. Bhaktivedanta Swami Prabhupada

Nearly five hundred years after Lord Caitanya Mahaprabhu walked among us, the *Sri Siksastaka* verses continue to lead all Vaisnavas ever deeper into the science and experience of pure, spontaneous and enveloping love of God.

His Holiness Bhakti-Tirtha Swami explores these verses from a contemporary perspective and helps modern devotees derive strength and realization from this timeless message, while reminding us of the important role we must play in carrying Lord Caitanya's legacy to future generations.

Order on the web at **www.ifast.net**

Reflections on Sacred Teachings

Volume Two: Madhurya-Kadambini

The Sweetness of Devotion

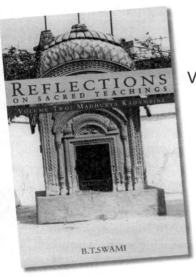

by B.T. Swami
(Swami Krishnapada)

$14.95, softbound ISBN #1-885414-14-5
244 pages

"Srila Visvanatha Cakravarti has given us a detailed analysis of the obstructions to our individual and collective devotional service. He has also given us a sublime outline of the stages of progress up to *prema*. Now the challenge is before each of us to fully use what he has given us. How blessed we all are to receive this opportunity through the blueprints given by such great *acaryas*, to facilitate us in returning back to the realm of pure, enchanting, enduring and animated love."

The Bhakti Trilogy is one of the great works of Visvanatha Cakravarti and his first presentation is the *Madhurya-Kadambini*. The word *kadambini* means a long bank of clouds that are showering *madhurya*, the sweetness of devotion. These clouds manifest over the environment to shower the *madhurya* and extinguish the blazing forest fire of material attraction and attachments. His Holiness Bhakti-Tirtha Swami explores these verses as a way of reminding the reader how such mentors and their teachings, although ancient, are as relevant now as they were in the past. Let the *madhurya*, the sweetness of devotion, shower us all as we take shelter of Srila Visvanatha Cakravarti Thakura's unlimited mercy.

Order on the web at **www.ifast.net**

Reflections on Sacred Teachings

Volume Three: Harinama Cintamani

The Holy Name Is The Key

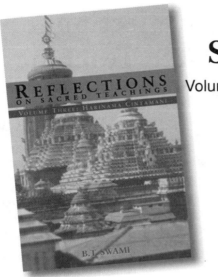

by B.T. Swami
(Swami Krishnapada)

$14.95, softbound ISBN #1-885414-15-3

"*Sri Harinama Cintamani* is the extraordinary conversation between the Supreme Lord Sri Caitanya Mahaprabhu and His devotee Srila Haridasa Thakura on the potency and efficacy of the holy name. His Holiness Bhakti-Tirtha Swami, a devout spiritual teacher in the Vaisnava line, leads us through the *Sri Harinama Cintamani* step-by-step, and enables us to hold onto the key of the holy name, unlocking the mysteries of our own pure and effulgent qualities. Srila Haridasa explains that the holy name will reach out—in spite of all the barriers and formalities—to the person who grabs and holds onto it.

"In previous ages, a person could reach perfection through meditation, temple worship or *yajnas* but in Kali-yuga, we cannot even perform one of the nine-fold activities nicely. Although just one of these nine activities can result in full love of Godhead, we engage in all nine and still have problems. Fortunately Srila Haridasa reveals the holy name as a source of hope in spite of the constant challenges in this Kali-yuga."

—*excerpts from Harinama Cintamani*

Order on the web at **www.ifast.net**

Order Form

ITEM		QUANT. TOTAL
• **Leadership for an Age of Higher Consciousness, Vol. I**	hardbound	$23.00 x __ = _____
	softbound	$14.95 x __ = _____
• **Leadership for an Age of Higher Consciousness, Vol. II**	hardbound	$23.00 x __ = _____
	softbound	$14.95 x __ = _____
• **Spiritual Warrior, Vol. I**	hardbound	
	softbound	$12.95 x __ = _____
• **Spiritual Warrior, Vol. II**	hardbound	$20.00 x __ = _____
	softbound	$12.95 x __ = _____
• **Spiritual Warrior, Vol. II Audio Tapes and CD set**	10 tapes	$45.00 x __ = _____
	9 CDs	$60.00 x __ = _____
• **Spiritual Warrior, Vol. III**	hardbound	$23.00 x __ = _____
	softbound	$14.95 x __ = _____
• **The Beggar, Vol. I**	hardbound	
	softbound	$11.95 x __ = _____
• **The Beggar, Vol. I Audio Tape set**	6 tapes	$28.00 x __ = _____
• **The Beggar, Vol. II**	softbound	$11.95 x __ = _____
	hardbound	
• **The Beggar, Vol. III**	softbound	$12.95 x __ = _____
	hardbound	
• **Reflections on Sacred Teachings, Vol. I**	softbound	$14.95 x __ = _____
• **Reflections on Sacred Teachings, Vol. II**	softbound	$14.95 x __ = _____
• **Reflections on Sacred Teachings, Vol. III**	softbound	$14.95 x __ = _____
	Subtotal	
	Shipping & Handling	
	Total	

○ I'd like more information on other books, CDs, audiotapes and videotapes from HNP.

Name: _____

Address: _____

City: _____ State: _____ Zip: _____

Daytime Phone: _____ Evening Phone: _____

Email Address: _____

Shipping and handling: **USA:** $5.00 for first book and $1.75 for each additional book. Air mail per book (USA only): $5.00. **Outside of the USA:** $8.00 for first book and $4.00 for each additional book. Surface shipping may take 3-4 weeks. Foreign orders: please allow 6-8 weeks for delivery.

Internet: www.ifast.net/hnp
Mail: Hari-Nama Press, PO Box 76451, Washington DC 20013